Visual Basic 2005 Express
for Beginners

Other Title by this Author

BP535   PC Interfacing using USB

Other Titles of Interest

BP554   Getting Started in Java
BP562   Getting Started with Java Applets

Visual Basic 2005 Express for Beginners

Peter Bates

Bernard Babani (publishing) Ltd
The Grampians
Shepherds Bush Road
London W6 7NF
England
www.babanibooks.com

Please note

Although every care has been taken with the production of this book to ensure that any programs contained herewith, operate in a correct and safe manner the Publisher and Author do not accept responsibility in any way for the failure (including fault in design) of any program to work correctly or to cause damage to any equipment that it may be connected to or used in conjunction with, or in respect of any other damage or injury that may be caused.

Notice is also given that if any equipment or software that is still under warranty is modified in any way then that warranty may be void.

At the time of writing Visual Basic 2005 Express was available as a free download from Microsoft's web site. This offer, of course, could be subject to change or withdrawal.

© 2006 BERNARD BABANI (publishing) LTD

First Published – October 2006

British Library Cataloguing in Publication Data
A catalogue record for this book is available from the British Library

ISBN 978-0-85934-570-5

Cover Design by Gregor Arthur
Printed and bound in Great Britain by CPD (Wales) Ltd, Ebbw Vale

To Margaret and Victoria

Preface

Visual Basic has been around for many years and has established a reputation as a programming language that produces professional Windows software. Its roots were in BASIC and it has come up via GWBasic and Microsoft's QuickBasic. Visual Basic did take a time to learn and perhaps was not the relatively easy programming language that beginners found BASIC to be. Nevertheless people adopted Visual Basic and despite its shortcoming in not being a structured programming language, it gained popularity and is widely used.

Visual Basic.NET broke the Visual Basic mould. The .NET version which appeared in 2003 was a structured language and most importantly it was an Object Orientated Programming (OOP) language. This development was significant as it meant that users had to be far more precise in their design of programs and in fact it necessitated careful consideration of a program design before it was committed to the keyboard. This OOP approach for Visual Basic has been maintained in the 2005 edition which has appeared in different varieties such as Standard, Professional and Team. Perhaps the most significant version is the Express which has broken new ground by being available as a free download from the Microsoft web site. Anyone who masters Visual Basic 2005 Express will find the transition to C, C++ and Java far less painful than the equivalent move from the original Visual Basic. On the downside learning Visual Basic 2005 Express either from scratch or from a knowledge of Visual Basic is quite a difficult task. This book has been designed and written to help with this process.

Each chapter in *Visual Basic 2005 Express for Beginners* concentrates on a particular theme and ensures that you obtain a thorough understanding of its meaning and application. The book has been designed to cover most aspects of the language that a beginner will need to write a program that will actually work. All the programs written in this book have been tried and tested and are well commented. Comments can appear to double the length of a program but are essential for both the author of the program and for anyone else who wishes to use it. I will not blame you if you omit the comments on first copying the programs in this book as you will be anxious to see whether or not the program will actually run but please when you start producing your own programs add the comments as you go along. It will have meant that you have understood the philosophy of this book which is that programs are designed, not just produced in an *ad hoc* way.

The book starts off with describing how to download Visual Basic 2005 Express from the web and then to load it on to your computer. It then deals with one its most difficult aspects, the Integrated Development Environment (IDE) which is its main screen. The next two chapters introduce the various parts of writing very simple programs and ensuring that you can find your way around the IDE. This process is reinforced in Chapter 4 when the properties of controls are encountered and you are given the opportunity to write your own programs.

Chapter 5 ventures into the automatic operation of programs by introducing the timer and a For...Next loop. Chapter 6 then digresses into how the Picture box can be used to display images and short animations but this is to enable you to plot graphs in Chapter 7. Chapter 8 then investigates how files can be used in different ways to store text and data and Chapter 9 returns to plotting data by looking at how bar and pie charts can be created.

As this book is designed to get you up and running with writing your own programs, Chapter 10 deals with how to debug your programs. By this time you should have gained confidence in writing programs and not be scared off by some of the terminology that is used in the language.

Visual Basic 2005 Express is a stepping stone to Visual Basic 2005 Standard and beyond. It will help to make the transition easier to the new versions of Visual Basic as they appear at regular intervals in the future.

Visual Basic 2005 Express will not make you an expert programmer but it will start you off in a gentle way. It will introduce the terminology that is used when it is really required. Most importantly it will provide you with programs that you can test now and come back to later when you have more experience. This book will provide a springboard to the more advanced books that are available. The main thing is that you learn how to program in Visual Basic 2005 Express and you enjoy it. If you can do that and you want to write more programs in the future, this book has achieved its aims.

Peter Bates
Preston
August 2006

About the Author

Peter Bates is currently the Course Leader of the MSc in Virtual Instrumentation in the Department of Physics, Astronomy and Mathematics at the University of Central Lancashire, Preston, UK. He is a physics graduate who went on to obtain a PhD in solid-state physics from Bangor University and in over 30 years he has taught physics, solid-state physics and microcomputer interfacing at all levels from A-level through to postgraduate. His interest in electronics developed as a consequence of being asked to teach the subject in 1974 when he was appointed to the Department of Physics at Preston Polytechnic.

Peter's expertise in interfacing sensors, transducers and instruments to computers was the foundation of the MSc in Virtual Instrumentation in which he is responsible for teaching fundamental interfacing and virtual instrumentation using Microsoft Visual Basic and National Instruments LabVIEW.

His hobbies are quite diverse ranging from hi-fi and music to DIY and gardening.

Trademarks

Microsoft, Windows XP, Visual Basic, Visual Basic.NET, Visual Basic 2005, Visual Basic 2005 Express and Excel are either registered trademarks or trademarks of the Microsoft Corporation.

All other brand and product names used in this book are recognized trademarks, or registered trademarks of their respective companies. There is no intent to use any trademarks generically and readers should investigate ownership of a trademark before using it for any purpose.

Contents

1

Getting Started 1

Installation 1
Starting up Visual Basic 2005 Express 2
Obtaining the default IDE 5
Features of the IDE 6
The Tool Windows 6
How to customise the IDE 7
Exercise 1.1 8
A closer look at the Tool Windows 8
The Toolbox 8
The Solution Explorer 10
The Properties Window 12
Help 12
Exercise 1.2 13
Making the Form larger 14
Summary 14

2

Our First Project 15

Some thoughts about programming 15
Example 2.1 16
Typing in the Program 17
Running the Program 24
What really happens when the Start button is pressed? 25
Closing the Project 25
Exercise 2.1 28
Summary 28

3

The Variable Parameter 29

What are Variable Parameters? 29
Example 3.1 30
Step 1 Designing the Form 30
Step 2 Setting the Properties of the Controls 32
Step 3 Writing the Code 33
Step 4 Running the Project 38
Step 5 Saving the Project 40
Exercise 3.1 41
Summary 41

4

Changing Properties 43

Another look at the Toolbox 44
Example 4.1 45
Changing the Properties 45
Adding the Code 46
Running the Program 48
Exercises 49
Exercise 4.1 49
Exercise 4.2 49
Summary 50

5

A Loop and Timer 51

Example 5.1 52
The Code 54
Running the Program 57

Exercise 5.1 59
Exercise 5.2 59
Example 5.2 60
Making a Copy of Example 5.1 Project 60
Creating Example 5.2 64
The Code 66
Running Example 5.2 68
Summary 69

6

Picture Boxes 71

Images 71
Example 6.1 72
The Code 73
Running the Program 74
Animation 78
Example 6.2 78
Exercise 6.1 78
Adding the Images 79
Exercise 6.2 82
The Code 82
Running Example 6.2 83
Example 6.3 84
Traffic Lights 84
The Form 84
The Code 86
Exercise 6.3 89
Running Example 6.3 89
Improving Example 6.3 90
Summary 92

7

Graphs 93

The Picture box 93

The Pixel	93
The Graph	94
The Scale	94
Line drawing	95
Example 7.1	96
The Code	96
Exercise 7.1	101
The Sine Wave	102
Example 7.2	103
Example 7.3	105
The Code	106
Running Example 7.3	109
Plotting Acquired Data	110
Example 7.4	111
The Form	111
Exercise 7.2	111
The Code	111
Exercise 7.3	113
Exercise 7.4	114
Running Example 7.4	115
Exercise 7.5	115
Summary	115

8

Files 117

What are Files?	117
Preparing to store Data	118
System.IO Namespace	118
Example 8.1	119
The Code	119
Analysing the Code	120
Running Example 8.1	122
Checking the Data on File	123
Example 8.2	123
The Code	124
Running Example 8.2	125
Exercise 8.1	126
Handling Numerical Data	126
Arrays	126

Example 8.3 127
The Code 128
Running Example 8.3 131
Example 8.4 132
The Code 133
Running Example 8.4 135
Storing Data in an alternative form 136
Example 8.5 136
The Code 137
Running Example 8.5 139
Example 8.6 140
The Code 141
Exercise 8.2 142
Running Example 8.6 142
Exercise 8.3 143
Summary 143

9

Bar and Pies 145

Example 9.1 145
The Code 146
Testing the Code 150
Testing the Program 160
Autoscaling Example 9.1 161
Exercise 9.1 162
Example 9.2 162
The Code 163
Testing for Colour 166
Drawing the Pie Chart 167
Exercise 9.2 169
Running Example 9.2 170
Exercise 9.3 171
Summary 171

10

Debugging 173
Errors 173
How to start Debugging..173
The IDE Menu..174
The Debug Toolbar...174
Stopping the Program 175
What to do when the Program stops 176
Keeping the Program running 177
Step Into..177
Step Over..177
Step Out..177
Managing Breakpoints 177
Debugging Windows 178
The Watch Window 178
The Immediate Window..180
Summary...182

Bibliography 183

Appendix..185
What you learn from each Example 185
Example 2.1 My First program 186
Example 3.1 Send & Receive...187
Example 4.1 Scrollbar multiplier 188
Example 5.1 Random Numbers 190
Example 5.2 Random Numbers – timed 192
Example 6.1 Bitmap images...194
Example 6.2 Icons..196
Example 6.3 Traffic lights 197
Example 7.1 Graph axes 199
Example 7.2 Sine wave graph..201
Example 7.3 Sine wave graph (Variable A & f) 203
Example 7.4 Random number graph 206
Example 8.1 File writer...210
Example 8.2 File reader 212

Example 8.3 Random number writer 214
Example 8.4 Random number reader 217
Example 8.5 Random number writer II 219
Example 8.6 Random number reader II 222
Example 9.1 Dice counter 224
Example 9.2 Colour mixing 230

Index 235

1
Getting Started

Microsoft Visual Basic 2005 is the latest version of Visual Basic. It continues the object-orientated programming features of the .NET version which appeared in 2003. This means that it is quite different from the versions of Visual Basic which first appeared in the 1990s and culminated in Visual Basic 6. All these different types of Visual Basic retain some of the features of the old BASIC that has been around since the 1970s but it does mean that even experienced Visual Basic programmers have had to learn some new techniques. Providing they are prepared to be flexible it is not too onerous a task to become conversant with Visual Basic 2005 fairly quickly.

This short book is designed to get you started and for you to learn the latest version of Visual Basic by the best possible method and that is by doing examples. This should then be the springboard for you to write your own programs. We shall start by initially reviewing how the software is installed and then spend the rest of this chapter showing how the Visual Basic 2005 screen can be arranged.

Installation

This book is based upon the Visual Basic 2005 Express edition. This is the free downloadable version that is obtained from the Microsoft web site. It contains a great deal of the features of Visual Basic 2005 Professional and as far as the examples in this book are concerned they are a good introduction to either version.

Visual Basic 2005 Express can be accessed from the Microsoft web site:
http://msdn.microsoft.com/vstudio/express/vb/

This offers a direct download facility or the opportunity to save the software on to a CD-ROM by following the manual installation instructions. If you are relatively inexperienced in downloading software from the web choose the former method. The manual method involves saving the software in either .img or .iso format and then burning it to a CD-ROM using either an IMG or ISO extractor which again can be downloaded from the web by searching using Google or another search engine.

1 Getting Started

Before you proceed with the download check that your computer meets the specifications required. This usually means that the processor is adequate, there is sufficient hard drive space available and that the operating system, i.e. Windows 2000, Windows XP, meets the necessary requirements. It is also necessary to have Microsoft Office 2003 installed. Sometimes there is a requirement that the appropriate Service Pack is also installed and it may be necessary to go to the Microsoft Service Pack site:

http://support.microsoft.com/gp/sp/

If either of these methods of obtaining Visual Basic Express fails, it is possible to obtain it from computer software dealers (at a small charge) or sometimes it is available in the free software given away in the monthly computer magazines.

Let us now presume that you have Visual Basic 2005 Express software. Either you have followed the download installation instructions or inserted the CD-ROM into the PC and obtained the screen shown in Figure 1.1.

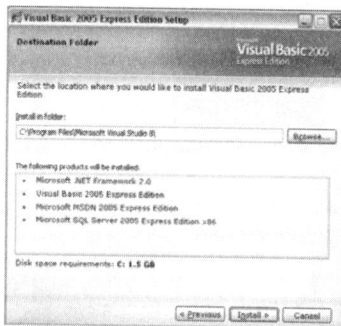

Figure 1.1 Visual Basic 2005 Express installation instructions

It is a case of right-clicking on *Install* and following the instructions.

Starting up Visual Basic 2005 Express

Visual Basic 2005 Express is started up in the same way as any software package on Windows XP. It is a case of going to **Start** on the bottom left-hand corner of the screen and selecting **All Programs**.

Getting Started 1

Move the mouse pointer over the list and select *Microsoft Visual Basic 2005 Express* Edition in the main menu (Figure 1.2).

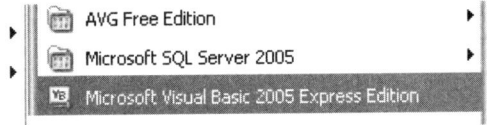

Figure 1.2 Selecting Visual Basic 2005 Express

The software will initially configure the environment (Figure 1.3).

Figure 1.3 Visual Basic 2005 Express configuration

This configuration only occurs on the first time of using Visual Basic 2005 Express and then the opening window appears (Figure 1.4).

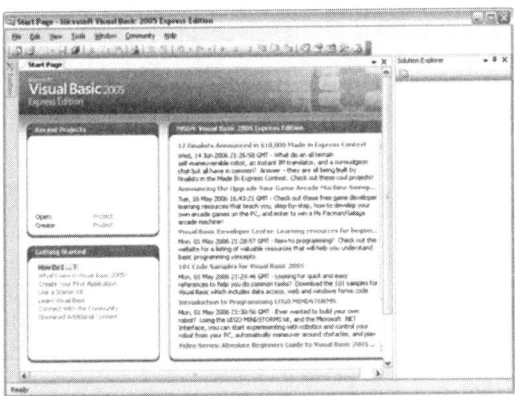

Figure 1.4 The Visual Basic 2005 Express Project opening window

Click *Create: Project...* to obtain the **New Project** menu (Figure 1.5).

1 Getting Started

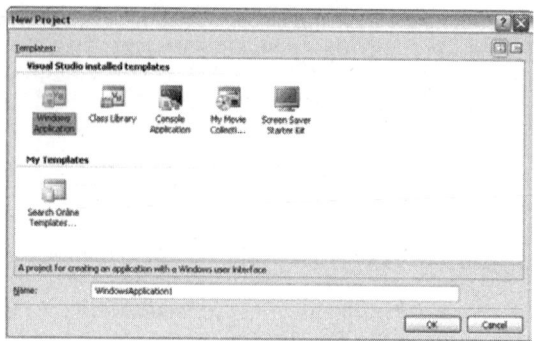

Figure 1.5 The New Project menu

Click *Windows Applications* and select a suitable Project name, e.g. *WindowsApplications1*. Then click *OK*.

This will bring up the Visual Basic 2005 Express Integrated Development Environment (IDE). The screen that you obtain may differ from Figure 1.6 and from any others that are shown in similar textbooks. This ability to customise the IDE is an important feature of Visual Basic 2005 Express.

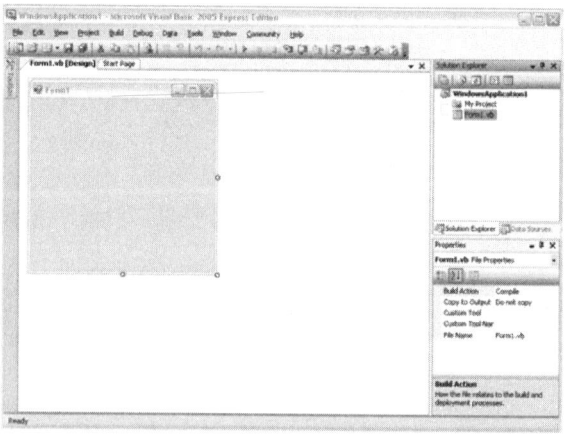

Figure 1.6 The Visual Basic 2005 Express IDE

Getting Started 1

The IDE shown in Figure 1.6 is the default setting. The IDE contains two types of windows; tool windows and document windows. We shall look at the two types later but for the present let us concentrate on ensuring that we all start with the same IDE configuration.

Obtaining the default IDE

This is obtained by clicking on **Window>Reset Window Layout** as shown in Figure 1.7.

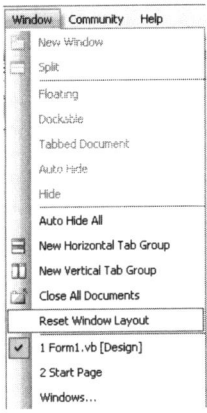

Figure 1.7 The Window menu

Click on *Reset Window Layout* and the following message box appears (Figure 1.8).

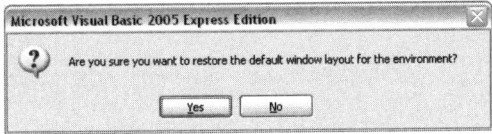

Figure 1.8 The warning message box

This message box simply warns you that your current Window's configuration will change but be assured your program will be unaffected.

1 Getting Started

Press *Yes* to clear the message box and the default window should now appear.

Features of the IDE

You can see that the IDE is similar in layout to many other Microsoft applications. There is a Menu bar and a Toolbar. There are also Tool Windows and Document Windows.

Document Windows are created when files are opened or created. The choice is between Multiple Document Interface (MDI) or Tabbed Documents, and it is in this latter mode that we shall operate for the examples in this book.

Figure 1.9 identifies the various features of the IDE.

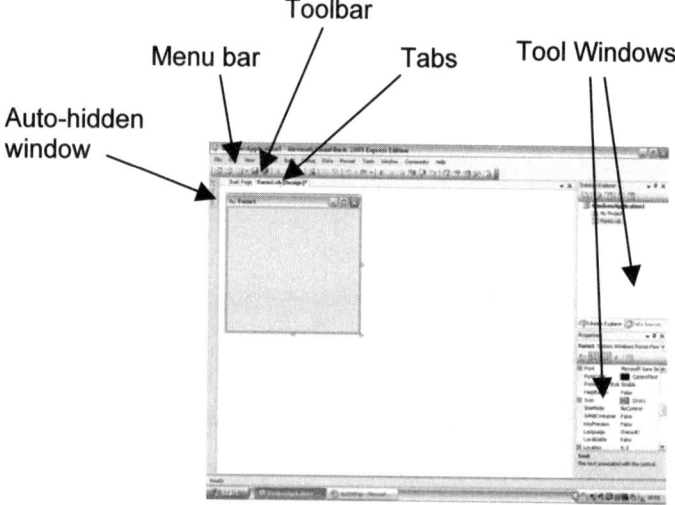

Figure 1.9 The IDE features

The Tool Windows

There are a number of Tool Windows and they can be accessed from the **View** menu on the Menu bar (Figure 1.10).

Getting Started 1

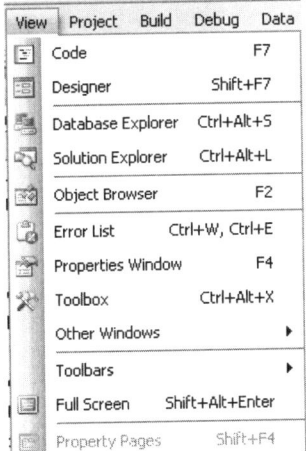

Figure 1.10 The View menu

The Tool Windows that are of use to us are:

    Solution Explorer
    Properties Window
    Toolbox

You will see that these are the ones that are already on the default IDE.

How to customise the IDE

The Tool Windows can be moved. Right-clicking on them reveals the options (Figure 1.11).

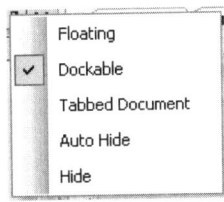

Figure 1.11 The Tool Window move options

1 Getting Started

This means that the Tool Windows can:

1. float
2. dock against the edges of the IDE
3. be tabbed
4. show or hide automatically
5. be hidden

Figure 1.9 showed examples of these.

Exercise 1.1

Try different settings for the Tool Windows to see how they behave.
Check File, Edit, View, etc., in the Menu Bar to see what can be done with the IDE.
Go back to the Default setting of Figure 1.6 when you have become familiar with the IDE.

A closer look at the Tool Windows

Let us now look at the Tool Windows to prepare ourselves to write a program. We shall look at the left-hand side of the IDE initially and then at the other side later.

The Toolbox

This is situated at the left-hand side of the IDE window. When the Toolbox icon is clicked the Toolbox will expand as in Figure 1.12.

Getting Started 1

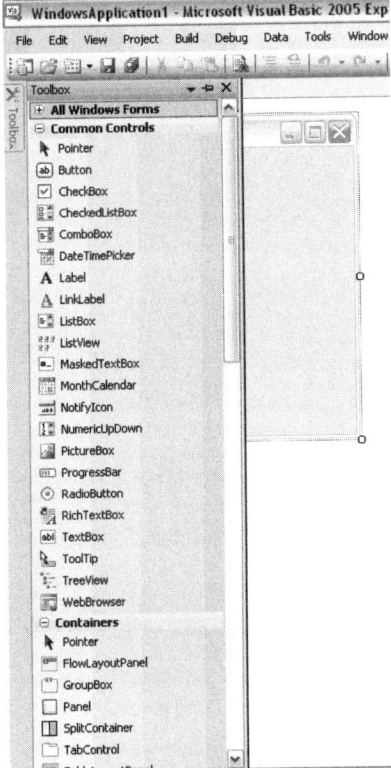

Figure 1.12 The Toolbox

The Toolbox can be shown and hidden at will by clicking on the Toolbox tab. You will notice that the Form window which is important to us for preparing the program is partially obscured. This may be easily remedied by clicking on the thumb pin on the Toolbox toolbar. When this is done, the Form and Toolbox take up the positions shown in Figure 1.13.

1 Getting Started

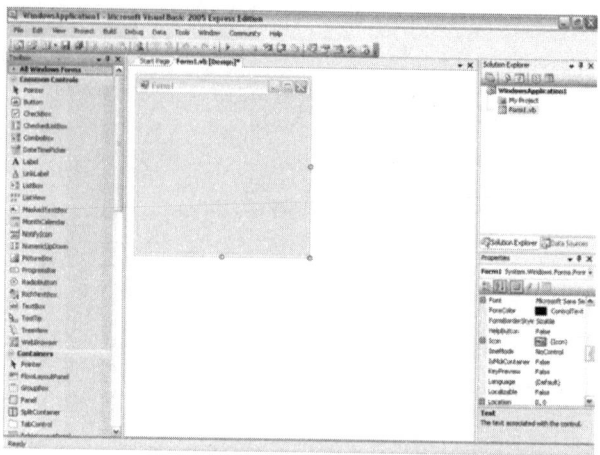

Figure 1.13 The Form and Toolbox in working positions

It is now possible to click on a tool in the Toolbox and then drag it on to the Form.

The Solution Explorer

This is situated on the right-hand side and is the uppermost of the two windows (Figure 1.14)

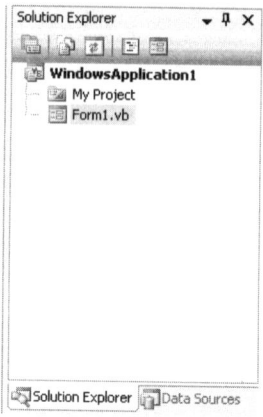

Figure 1.14 The Solution Explorer

Getting Started 1

This window shows the files that are contained in the Project. When the Form is highlighted it is possible to switch between the Form and the Program by pressing either of the icons in the Toolbar (Figure 1.15).

Figure 1.15 The Program or Form selection icons

You will notice that the Solution Explorer is tabbed (Figure 1.16).

Figure 1.16 The Solution Explorer/Data Sources tabs

The Data Sources (Figure 1.17) provides information about the places from which the application will obtain its data.

Figure 1.17 The Data Sources

If you click on *Add New Data Source...* you can select from *Database, Web Service or Object*. This is a little involved at this stage of our

1 Getting Started

introduction to Visual Basic 2005 Express but it will be more relevant as we become more experienced.

The Properties Window

When the Form or any Control that is placed on it is highlighted, the various properties are displayed in the Properties Window (Figure 1.18).

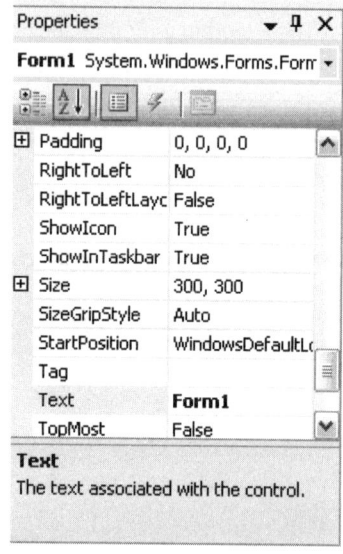

Figure 1.18 The Properties Window

We shall use the Properties Window often as we develop Projects. It enables us to customise a Form or Control and ensures that the Project will look and behave in the way we wish it to.

Help

The other feature of importance on the IDE is Help which is accessed from the Toolbar (Figure 1.19).

Getting Started 1

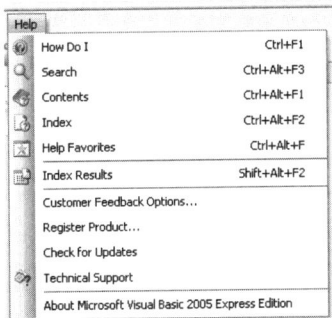

Figure 1.19 Dynamic Help

There are many different methods of Help and the choice is yours over which you choose. Figure 1.20 shows the *How Do I* Window.

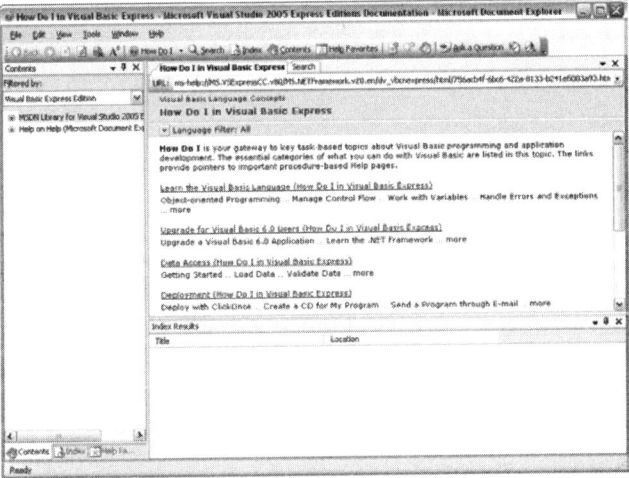

Figure 1.20 *How Do I* Help in action

Exercise 1.2

Investigate the different types of Help that are available in Visual Basic 2005 Express.

1 Getting Started

Making the Form larger

Sometimes it may be useful to make the Form larger. The increased space can be created by clicking the thumb pins of both the Solution Explorer and the Properties Windows so that they both become hidden (Figure 1.21).

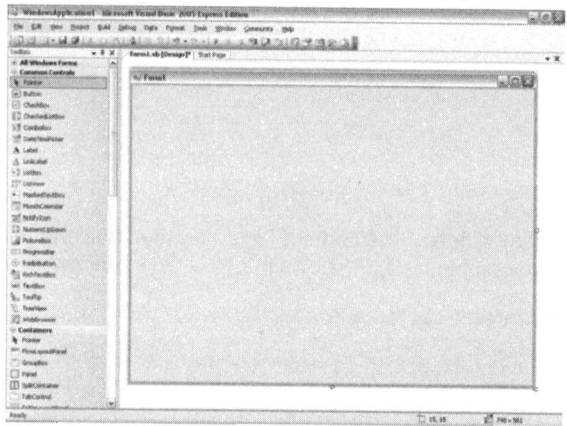

Figure 1.21 The Right-hand Tools Windows hidden

Summary

This chapter has shown you how the Visual Basic 2005 Express is set up. It has indicated how Visual Basic 2005 Express is installed and then how the default window is retrieved. This is very important as the Tool Windows can become quite disorganised as you develop a complicated Project and it is reassuring that a sense of order is only a few key strokes away.

You have also been given the opportunity to become familiar with the most common Tool Windows and the next task is to a write a simple Visual Basic 2005 Express program that will enable us to develop more advanced programs in the future.

2
Our First Project

As you will have gathered from Chapter 1 Visual Basic 2005 Express programs are called projects which are made up of a number of files. This is in line with other structured and object orientated programming languages like C++ and Java. It is a long way from the original BASIC programs which consisted normally of a very long file with a .bas extension but is more typical of earlier versions of Visual Basic which were made up of Forms and Modules.

When a Visual Basic 2005 Express project is created it is really creating a folder into which a collection of different files will be placed. This is very similar to C projects and does indicate that there will be similarities in the way the programs are going to be written. The similarities soon become obvious when you start as it will be necessary to declare all the parameters that you use. It will be found to extend as the program increases in size but the one reassuring fact is that Microsoft provides help as you type in your lines of code. This will be apparent in the first program that we shall write.

Some thoughts about programming

This may be your very first program or you may be an experienced programmer who is moving over to Visual Basic 2005 Express from earlier versions of Visual Basic or some other language. Whichever one of these persons you are it is vitally important to consider what you are doing.

You are going to spend a certain amount of time keying in lines of code which hopefully will produce the desired result the first time you run the program. There are some people who can sit down at a piano and play a Beethoven sonata straight off after only hearing it once before. Rarely in the world of computing can someone write a lengthy computer program and for it to work first time it runs. We mere mortals need to think what the program has to do and then plan it before we even start to type at the computer keyboard. This is true for a simple program up to the more advanced ones that we shall consider later in this book.

2 Our First Project

In fact there are some rules which we should follow when we write programs. Very simply they are:

1. Design the program
2. Type in the program
3. Save the program
4. Run the program
5. Debug the program (if necessary)

If you follow these rules you will find the whole task of programming less frustrating and your computer will benefit as you will treat it more kindly as it is behaving in the way that you want it to.

So let's get started.

Example 2.1

Before we can write the program we do need to know what the desired result will be. Once this has been achieved we need to decide the steps that will be required to get to that result. In fact we need to be able to describe the program in some detail and it is usually better to do this in a diagram rather than in words and this diagram is called a flowchart.

The first program we shall write is the classic "Hello world" program. This is the traditional program that most programmers learn in any new language that they encounter. In our case it will be the message that appears when the program is run and a button is pressed by the mouse on the monitor screen.

Figure 2.1 shows the flow chart which will be the basis of the program.

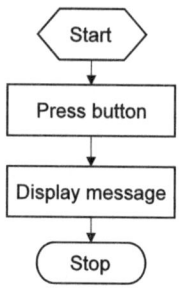

Figure 2.1 The flow chart

Our First Project 2

The next step is to put this into a program

Typing in the Program

This is the process with which you will become very familiar but we need to go through it step by step to start with to ensure that you understand why certain things are done.

We shall start off with a clean sheet so that this means starting up Visual Basic 2005 Express (Figure 2.2).

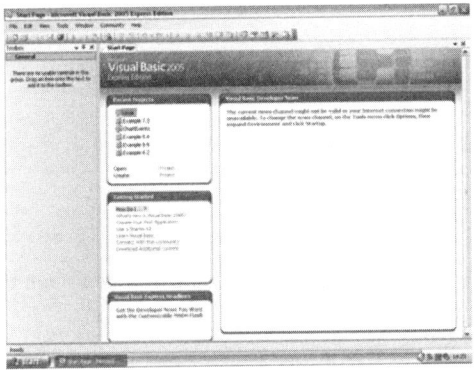

Figure 2.2 The Start Page

Select *New Project* from the File menu and the New Project window appears (Figure 2.3).

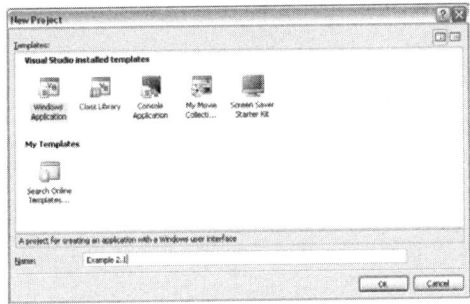

Figure 2.3 Naming the New Project

17

2 Our First Project

Our first project is going to be called Example 2.1. Therefore type in Example 2.1 into the Name textbox.

Click OK in the New Project Window and obtain the Visual Basic 2005 Express default page (Figure 2.4).

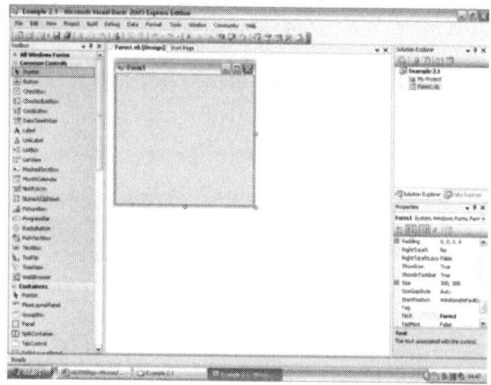

Figure 2.4 The Visual Basic 2005 Express default page

If the screen does not have the appearance of Figure 2.4 go back to Chapter 1 and refer to how it can be obtained.

The first stage of writing the program is to fill in the Form. This first program requires a Label, a Textbox and a Button. If you look at the Toolbox you will see these are distributed in alphabetical order in the Windows Forms list (Figure 2.5).

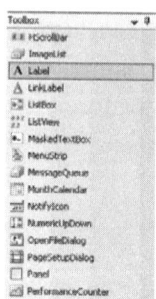

Figure 2.5 The Toolbox list

Our First Project   2

These will now need to be transferred on to the Form.

First of all highlight the Label and then position the pointer on the Form in a suitable place and draw out an appropriately sized rectangle (Figure 2.6).

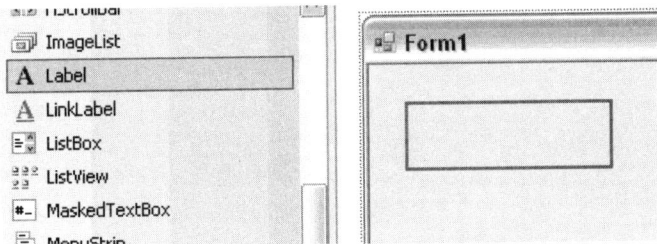

Figure 2.6 Drawing out the Label rectangle

Label1 will now be positioned on the Form (Figure 2.7).

Figure 2.7 Label1 on the Form

The Label rectangle can be resized and re-positioned using the mouse. The text in the Label box can also be changed.

This involves going to Text in the Properties Window (Figure 2.8) and typing in the appropriate word, e.g. Response.

2 Our First Project

Figure 2.8 Locating Text in the Properties Window

Response will now be the Label on the Form (Figure 2.9).

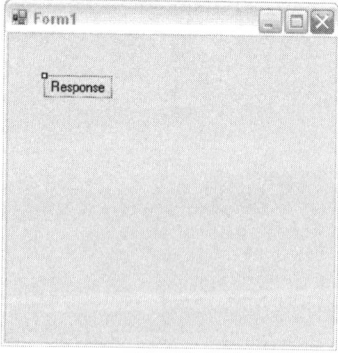

Figure 2.9 The new Label

The Label rectangle can be resized and the font type and size can be changed in the Font property of the Properties Window. Simply double-click on the three ellipses, i.e. ..., and obtain the Font dialog box (Figure 2.10).

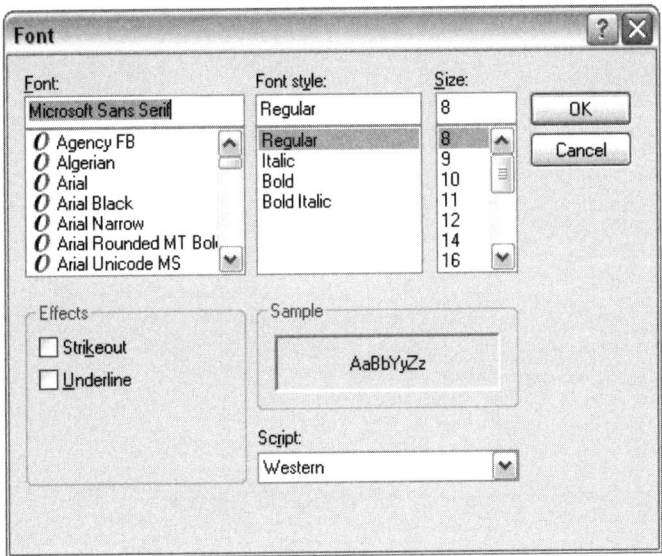

Figure 2.10 Changing the font type and size

This results in Figure 2.11.

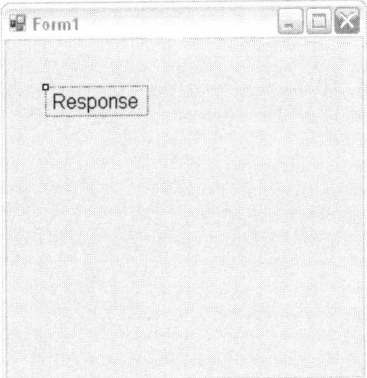

Figure 2.11 Effect of changing font type and size and resizing Label

Dealing with the Textbox and Button is a very similar process.

2 Our First Project

In the case of the Textbox, the Text property is cleared with the spacebar (Figure 2.12).

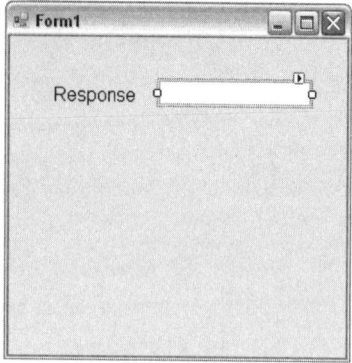

Figure 2.12 Adding the Textbox

The Button is placed below the Label and Textbox and the Text property is changed to *Press* (Figure 2.13).

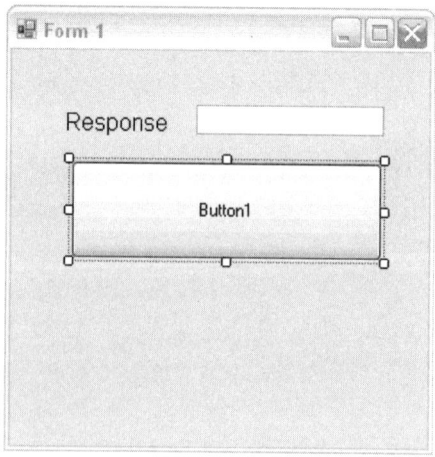

Figure 2.13 The *Press* Button

To complete the Form its own Text should be changed. For this example *My First Program* appears to be most appropriate.

Our First Project 2

The final act prior to writing any code is to adjust the size of the Form by dragging up the bottom of it so that the Form appears very much more compact (Figure 2.14).

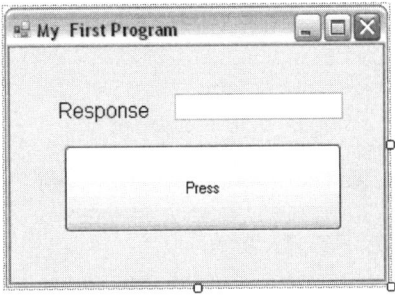

Figure 2.14 Final layout of the Form

Before we move any further it is worthwhile noting that the names of the Label, the Textbox and the Button are Label1, Textbox1 and Button1. Some programmers prefer to go into the Properties and change the Name property to something that may be regarded as more relevant, e.g. Button1 becomes Pressbutton. This is all a case of personal preference but all of the examples in this book will retain the names as provided by the software.

To add code to a particular control, e.g. the Press button, you double-click on the Button. The relevant portion of code then appears (Figure 2.15).

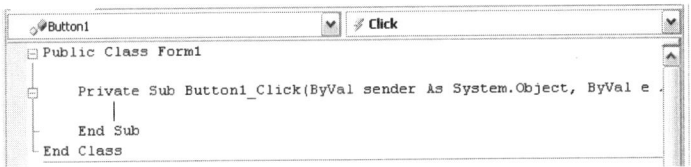

Figure 2.15 The Button code area

The statement :

Textbox1.Text="Hello world"

2 Our First Project

is typed between the two lines *Private Sub* and *End Sub* (Figure 2.16).

```
(General)                              (Declarations)
Public Class Form1

    Private Sub Button1_Click(ByVal sender As System.Object, ByVal e
        TextBox1.Text = "Hello World"
    End Sub
End Class
```

Figure 2.16 The added text

That is all we need, we now have to run the program.

Running the Program

The program can be run with either the code or the Form being shown. The process is activated by pressing the arrow icon located on the Menu Bar (Figure 2.17).

Figure 2.17 The Start button

When the Start button is pressed the Form code is compiled. This build process may take some time especially if there are errors which will appear in a window at the bottom of the screen. We shall deal with debugging a program in the next chapter but considering that we have three controls on the Form and only one line of code, the program should compile without any problem. Eventually the Form will appear in running mode (Figure 2.18).

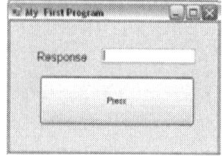

Figure 2.18 The Form running

When we click on the Press button, the words *Hello World* will appear in the text box (Figure 2.19). Your first Visual Basic 2005 Express program has run!

Our First Project 2

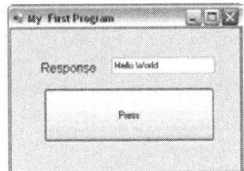

Figure 2.19 Showing that the program works

What really happens when the Start button is pressed?

When the Start button is pressed there is a short delay before the Form appears before you can activate the program, i.e. press the Press button. During this period of time the program is saved prior to it being checked before being compiled in code that the computer can actually run. The period of time can be shortened if you have already saved the program but there is the consolation that if the program fails to run properly such that the computer 'hangs', i.e. goes into suspended animation and has to be switched off in order to get it operational again, your program can be recovered prior to correction.

Closing the Project

To ensure that the process of closing the project takes place in a sensible way you should ensure that you close it before opening another one. The easiest one of performing the task is to select File>Close Project (Figure 2.20).

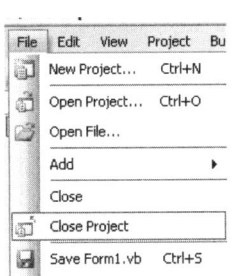

Figure 2.20 Closing the Project

2   Our First Project

You will then be prompted with the request shown in Figure 2.21.

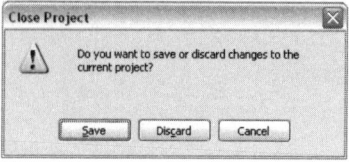

Figure 2.21 The Close Project message box

The choice is then yours. Presuming that you wish to retain your program you should click *Save*. This will then bring up the *Save Project* dialog box shown in Figure 2.22.

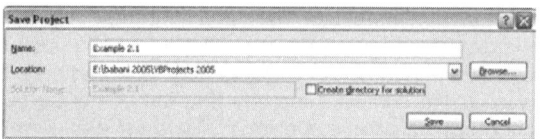

Figure 2.22 The Save Project dialog box

Our first project is called Example 2.1 and we shall put it into a folder called VBProjects. We shall put all our projects into this folder so that they are in one place and we can find them all easily in the future. It also makes it easier to archive all of the Visual Basic 2005 Express projects when you copy them on to a flash memory stick.

Therefore select Browse and the Project Location window shown in Figure 2.23 appears.

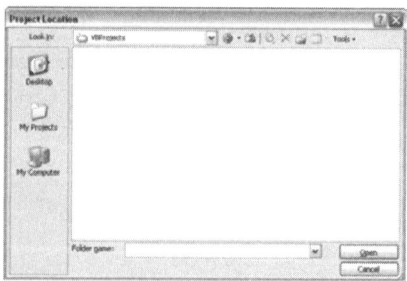

Figure 2.23 The Project Location window

Our First Project 2

Either locate the VBProjects folder or create it and bring it up as shown in Figure 2.23. Then click on *Open* to return to the Save Project dialog box (Figure 2.24).

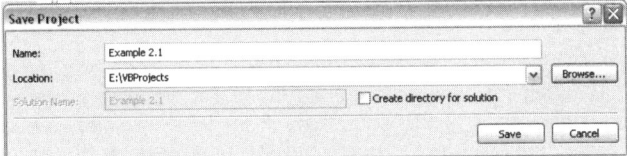

Figure 2.24 The completed Save Project dialog box

Do not check, i.e. tick, the *Create directory for solution* box.

Click on *Save* and the project will then save and close down.

To check what has been done, you should go into **My Computer** from the **Start** button on the Desktop and navigate to the VBProjects folder. If you go down a level to Example 2.1 you will find more folders at two different levels under Example 2.1 (Figure 2.25 and 2.26).

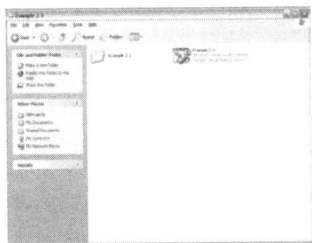

Figure 2.25 The upper level of Example 2.1 folder

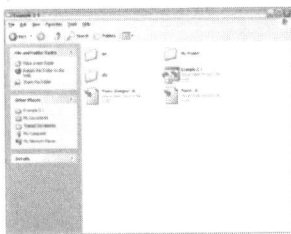

Figure 2.26 The lower level of Example 2.1 folder

2 Our First Project

The compilation and saving process results in several files being created and if you go into the folder you will see more folders and files than you had before the folder was first created during the *New Project* creation process.

It now becomes more obvious why a folder is created and used for a project. Everything is self-contained and can be easily copied and pasted elsewhere. This is something from which earlier versions of Visual Basic suffered in so much that the files were scattered around and invariably were lost when the file was taken to another computer.

Exercise 2.1

Reload Example 2.1. This will involve going to **File>Open** and then selecting the *VBProjects* folder. Select Example 2.1 and then select Example 2.1.vb at the next stage. Example 2.1 should then load.

Summary

This chapter has enabled you to write your first Visual Basic 2005 Express program. It may have appeared rather complicated but it has shown you the different steps required and explained why they have been undertaken.

You can be assured that the whole process will become second nature to you as you obtain more experience. The next chapter will introduce you to a more complicated program which may be more susceptible to error so that you can learn how to debug a program. This is when programming becomes exciting!

3
The Variable Parameter

We have now got our first program up and running and we have some knowledge of the basic features of Visual Basic 2005 Express. Let us move on to a slightly more advanced program and see how we can deal with errors that are caused by either us making mistakes as we type the program in or detecting those notorious bugs which appear for no apparent reason.

The steps that we shall take are:
1. Design a Form using the Form Window
2. Set the properties of the controls on the Form using the Properties Window
3. Write the code to respond to the actions in the Code Window
4. Run the project
5. Save the application

The program that we shall write is an extension of the *Hello World* program and will involve us typing in our name into a textbox and then pressing a button again to initiate a response. It will extend our understanding of Visual Basic 2005 Express by introducing something called a variable parameter. Variable parameters are used extensively in programs and enable such programs to become very versatile and powerful.

What are Variable Parameters?

These are symbols which can contain either numerical or alphabetical (character) information. In mathematics, algebra has equations which are made up of symbols which can represent numbers, e.g. $X + Y = 10$. X and Y are variable parameters which can have a range of numerical values provided the combination adds up to 10.

Similarly we may have a symbol which represents a character string, e.g. NA="John". This parameter may be used over and over again whenever the word *John* is required, e.g. in a document. In Visual Basic 2005 Express the word John is enclosed within inverted commas to ensure the computer knows that the 4 letters J, o, h and n are kept together.

3 The Variable Parameter

It would appear that variable parameters are simply either numerical or character strings but unfortunately that is far from being true. Numerical information can take several forms. It can be whole numbers (integers), numbers with decimal points (floating point) or currency. Within these categories there is further splitting up depending upon the range of numbers that can be accommodated by the particular type. Table 3.1 elaborates upon this point.

Variable Name	Format
Integer	-2,147,483,648 to 2,147,483,647
Long	-9,223,372,036,854,775,808 to 9,223,372,036,854,775,807
Short	-32,768 to 32,767
Single	-3.3E-38 to 3.37E+38
Double	-1.67E -308 to 2.67E+308
Currency	-9.22E+14 to 9.22E +14
Date	1 January 0001 to 31 December 9999
Boolean	True or False
Byte	0 to 255
String	Character string

Table 3.1 Format of variables

Example 3.1

This example will enable us to communicate with the PC and get a response from it.

Step 1 Designing the Form

Start up Visual Basic 2005 Express and select *New Project*. Call the project *Example 3.1* and save it in the folder where you are keeping your Visual Basic 2005 Express projects. This should be done every time as it ensures that you do not lose any of your work.

Click on **Save All** in the **File** menu (Figure 3.1).

The Variable Parameter   3

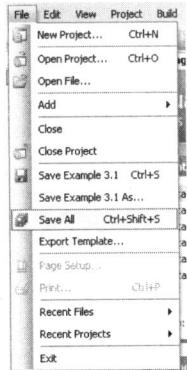

Figure 3.1 Highlighting Save All

The familiar Save Project dialog box will appear (Figure 3.2) which we can use in just the same way as we did in Chapter 2.

Figure 3.2 Saving Example 3.1

Now highlight Form1.vb in the Solution Explorer and obtain the Form window by clicking on the View Designer icon in the toolbar of the Solution Explorer window.

Place 2 Labels, 2 Textboxes and a Button on to the Form in the positions shown in Figure 3.3. There is no need to be too accurate with the positions as long as the Form has a similar layout.

The controls should be placed on the Form in the following order:

Label1
Label2
Textbox1
Textbox2
Button1
Form1

3 The Variable Parameter

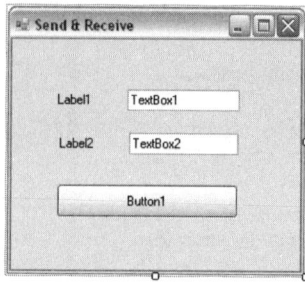

Figure 3.3 Example 3.1 Form

The program will work in the following way:
When the program is running you type your name into Textbox1 and then press the Button by clicking on it with the mouse. A response will appear in Textbox 2.

Step 2 Setting the Properties of the Controls

Labels and the Button on the Form and the Form itself have their Text properties changed. This is achieved by selecting the Text property in the relevant Property window and making the following changes:

Form1 – Change the Text to *Send & Receive*
Label1 – Change the Text to *Input your Name*
Label2 – Change the Text to *Response*
Button1 – Change the Text to *Press*

Figure 3.4 shows how the Form now appears.

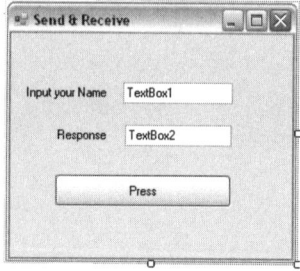

Figure 3.4 The completed Form

Step 3 Writing the Code

The next step is to add code to the Form. It is a case of selecting the Code window by clicking on the View Code icon in the Solution Explorer window.

The Form 1 box which is highlighted in Figure 3.5 is the Class Name box.

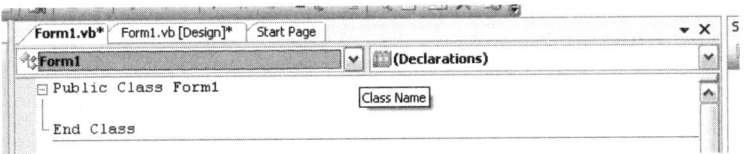

Figure 3.5 The View Class box highlighted

When this box is clicked the different Classes are revealed and you will see that they relate to the controls on the Form (Figure 3.6)

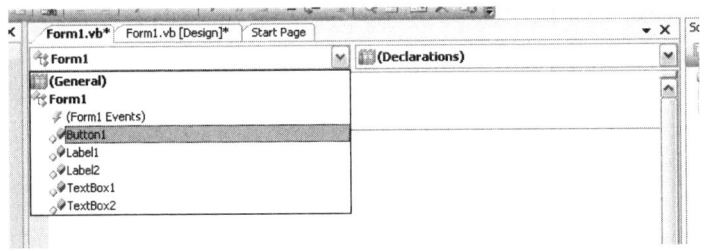

Figure 3.6 The Class Names revealed

Clicking on any of these Names will show the code associated with it. We are interested in Button1 so highlight Button1 and then determine the code we have to add in order for the button to react. This involves the Method Name box which lies to the right of the Class Names box in the Code window (Figure 3.7).

3 The Variable Parameter

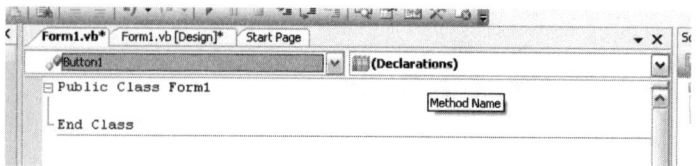

Figure 3.7 Identifying the Method Name box

When the Method Name box is clicked, all of the different actions are revealed (Figure 3.8).

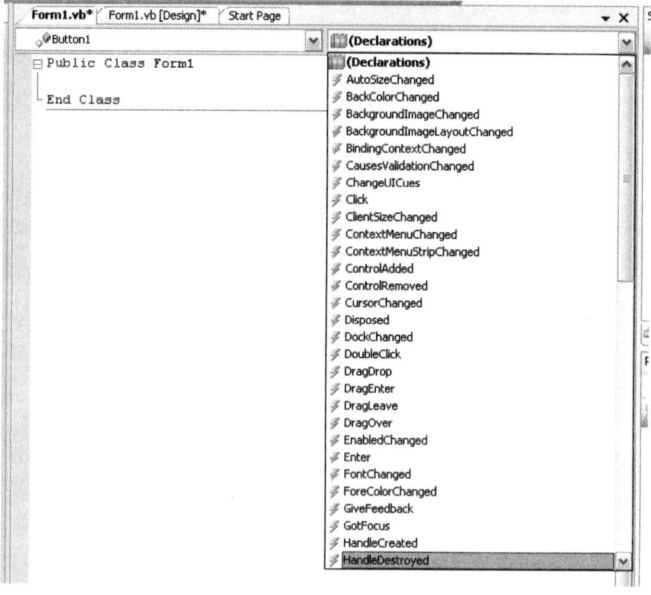

Figure 3.8 Selecting the appropriate Method

When *Click* is selected the Button1_Click code section appears (Figure 3.9).

The Variable Parameter   3

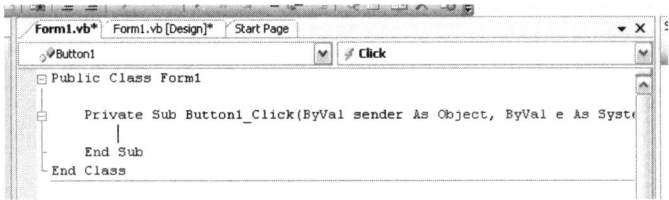

Figure 3.9 The Button1_Click code

This process may appear slower than the one adopted in Chapter 2 where the similar code section was activated by simply double-clicking on the control on the Form. Both methods are acceptable but the method described in this chapter shows all the different button actions that can be activated.

Before we add any code we can add a window to the IDE which will help as we go along. Click on **Error List** in the **View** menu (Figure 3.10).

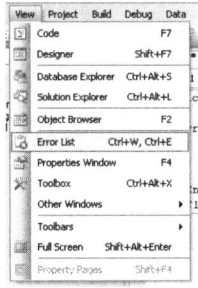

Figure 3.10 Accessing the Error List

The Error List will now appear at the bottom of the IDE screen (Figure 3.11).

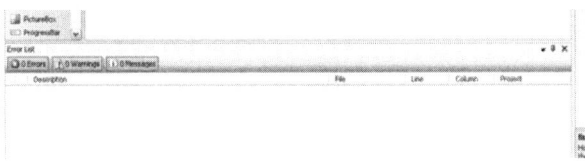

Figure 3.11 The Error List

35

3　The Variable Parameter

We now need to add some code and the text that needs to be typed is:

```
Private Sub Button1_Click(ByVal sender As Object, ByVal e As
 System.EventArgs) Handles Button1.Click

    NA = TextBox1.Text
    TextBox2.Text = "Hello " + NA

End Sub
```

The First line *Private....* And the last line *End Sub* are already written so that it is only the two middle lines you need to type in.

As you type in the words two events occurred which are quite important.

The first occurred after typing in NA. A blue wavy line appeared beneath the two letters and the statement shown in Figure 3.12 appears in the Error List at the bottom of the screen.

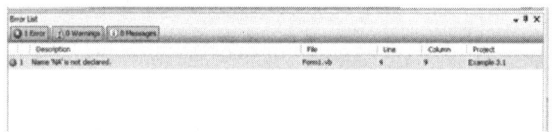

Figure 3.12 Documenting the errors

This shows that NA which is a variable parameter has not been declared and is the source of an error. This is a matter which we shall need to remedy.

The second event occurred as *Textbox1.* was typed in. Just as the point was typed in, the dialog box shown in Figure 3.13 appeared.

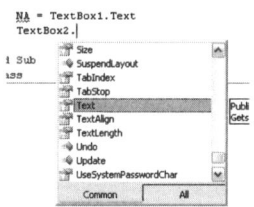

Figure 3.13 The Method dialog box

The Variable Parameter 3

The Method dialog box ensures that the correct activity is selected and saves any extra typing. It is very useful as it checks your own spelling and also determines whether or not a particular control is recognized within the project.

Once the two lines have been typed in we can turn our attention back to the variable parameter NA. In fact the error has been compounded because we have used NA twice within the program without it being compared.

NA has to be declared as a variable parameter. In fact as we wish to type a name in it, it has to be declared as a string.

Variables can be declared as either *Public* or *Private*. Public means that they can be seen both in the current Form and in any other Form and as a consequence they are placed at the top of the program. Private variables can either be restricted to the sub-routine in which they are placed or in a particular Form if they are placed at the top of it. The different ranges of visibility of a variable are referred to as the *scope* of a variable.

Returning back to our variable NA which will be declared as Private and placed at the very beginning of the program. This is in the Form Declaration section which is indicated by the Class Name and the Method Name boxes at the top of the Code window.

The additional program statement is:

| Private NA as String |

As you type the word String you will find the Tip window will come to your assistance to ensure that you use the correct term (Figure 3.14).

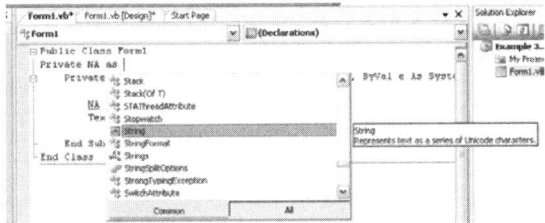

Figure 3.14 Typing in the Declaration

3   The Variable Parameter

The final part of inserting code involves setting up the two textboxes. These need to be cleared before running the program.

The following two lines of code achieve this:

```
Textbox1.Text=""
Textbox2.Text=""
```

The inverted commas with nothing between them are referred to as a null string. The question arises as to where in the program do we place them. We need to initialise the program each time the Form is loaded so the obvious place to put them is in the Form_Load section (Figure 3.15).

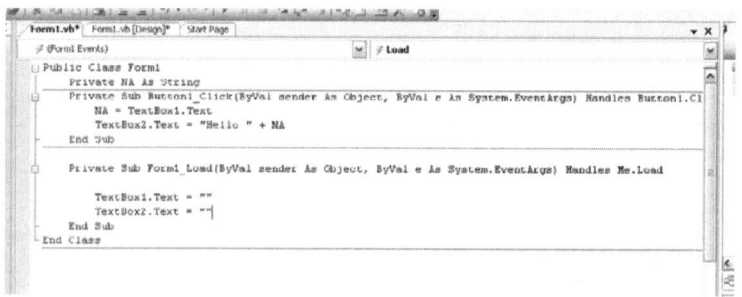

Figure 3.15 Inserting the two clear textboxes statements

The Form_Load section of code is accessed by selecting *Form1 Events* and *Load* in the Class Name and Method name boxes respectively.

The code is now ready and we need to test it.

Step 4 Running the Project

When the Run icon is clicked in the Toolbar, the Form will be built automatically. Hopefully there will be no errors as we should have picked them up earlier. If there are they will be displayed in the error Task List of Figure 3.12. If there are no errors the Form will appear as shown in Figure 3.16.

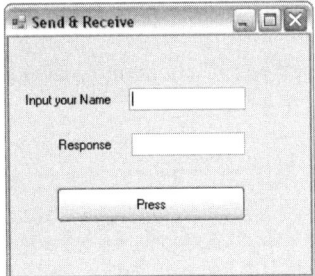

Figure 3.16 The Form running

To use the Form we simply type a name into the *Input your Name* textbox (Figure 3.17)

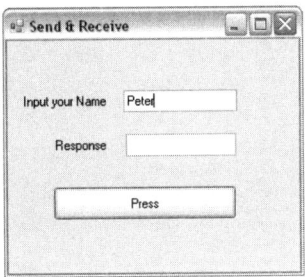

Figure 3.17 Entering a name

When the Press button is clicked, the response obtained is shown in Figure 3.18.

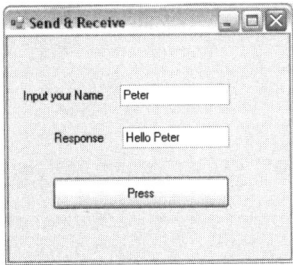

Figure 3.18 Obtaining the response

3 The Variable Parameter

It looks as if the desired result has been obtained and the program has performed as predicted.

Step 5 Saving the Project

An important feature of Visual Basic 2005 Express is that the various parts of the project are automatically saved when the Build process is activated either by selecting Build or Run.

Individual parts of the Project can be saved at any time by selecting Save, Save As or Save All as shown in Figure 3.19.

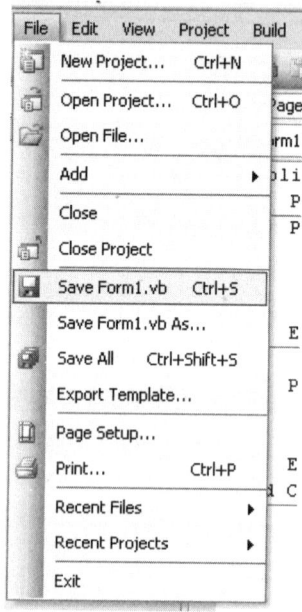

Figure 3.19 The various types of Save

The object of Save and Save As is dependent on what is highlighted in the Solutions Explorer window, i.e. Form 1.vb or Example 3.1.sln. This is useful as a project is developed so that it is possible to change names as you go along.

In Chapter 5 we shall consider how to copy folders and files and how to change their names. For the present time make sure you adhere to the following rule:

DO NOT CHANGE THE NAMES OF FILES OUTSIDE VISUAL BASIC 2005

If you do, you may have problems which are difficult to sort out.

Exercise 3.1

Rearrange the controls on the Form so that they are in an order in which a user may find them intuitively easier to use. This means that the controls may have additional labels attached to them such as Step 1, Step 2 and Step 3.

What effect does changing the positions of the controls and adding the numbers have upon the code that you have already written?

Summary

This chapter has shown how a typical Visual Basic 2005 Express program can be put together. It has illustrated the steps of designing the Form, setting the properties of the controls, adding the codes and then building the project during the Run process. It has also illustrated how important it is to make sure the Form is user friendly so that it is obvious to the user what needs to done before actioning the program, i.e. Fill in your name, press the button and wait for the response.

The next stage is to get to know more controls and write more complex programs.

3   The Variable Parameter

4
Changing Properties

If you look at the Toolbox you will find many different types of controls that you can use. We could go through them all but not only will you find the task bewildering but also you may find that you never actually use them. A better approach is to introduce them as and when they are needed. In this way you will discover what they are capable of doing at the appropriate time but also you will find out what Properties need to be set and how the Properties are changed when the program is running.

You now have some idea of how to put a Visual Basic 2005 Express project together so that we can introduce a few other techniques that we shall use as the book progresses. First of all we shall introduce two terms; Design time and Run time.

Design time is the period when you are putting together the program and you are placing controls on to the Form and altering the Properties. The Properties range from Text that is used on a Form, on a Button, in a Label, etc., to setting the physical size of the control according to its height and width.
This presetting of a Property can sometimes affect whether or not the program will ever start and we shall see examples of that in later chapters.

Run time is the time when the program is actually running and in this case the properties are altered under program control. We have already seen this in Chapter 3 where Textboxes had their text cleared as the Form was loaded. In fact changing Properties as the program runs is at the heart of the way that Visual Basic 2005 Express works.

Another technique we shall introduce is how the program will be introduced to you in this book. So far we have shown screen shots of the code and you should have found that it has not been too difficult to copy. However as the programs become more complex a clearer means of presentation is required. This problem is resolved by taking code in blocks and placing a frame around it and shading inside the frame. It should then be easy to see what you need to type into your program. Any code that does not require typing in will not be shaded. The only exceptions to this rule are the lines that appear automatically for a sub-routine, i.e. the first and last lines. These should appear only once in a sub-routine.

4 Changing Properties

Another addition we shall make to the code is the inclusion of *comment* statements. These are statements to help to explain what a particular line or chunk of code is trying to do. Programs should be well commented so that anybody looking at the code can understand what is being done. A comment statement can be preceded either by rem or more usually '. There are plenty of examples of this in the code examples in this and following chapters.

Our next program uses a scrollbar to supply a number into the input box. The number in the output box is the input number multiplied by a multiplier selected by one of the three Radio buttons (three buttons of which only one is active at any time). The input and output numbers change continuously as the scroll bar moves up and down.

So in this chapter we shall look at a program that does some simple calculation and then you will have the opportunity to test out your new-found skills in Visual Basic 2005 Express by trying two further Exercises.

Another look at the Toolbox

The controls we shall use in this program are Labels, Textboxes, a Scroll bar, a Group box and some Radio Buttons. These can all be located on the Toolbox shown in Figure 4.1.

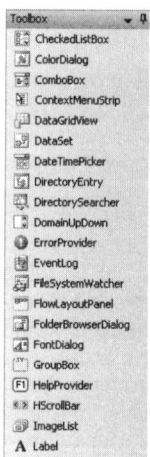

Figure 4.1 The Toolbox

Changing Properties 4

With all of these controls we shall be changing their Properties.

Example 4.1

Start up a New Project in Visual Basic 2005 Express and call it Example 4.1 and lay out the controls as shown in Figure 4.2.

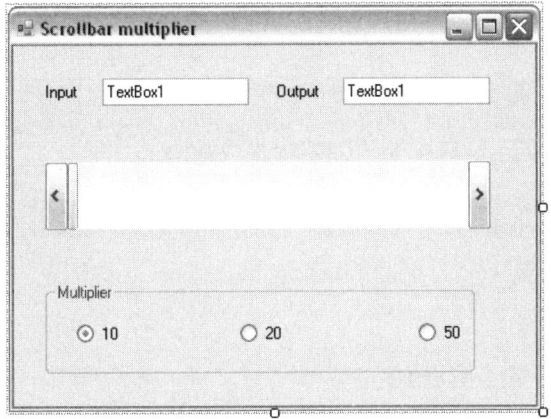

Figure 4.2 Layout of the Scrollbar multiplier Form

The three new controls that we have to consider are:

1. HScrollbar
2. Groupbox – this must be placed on the Form before the Radiobuttons
3. Radiobuttons x 3 – size these so that the Text is visible

The next stage is to ensure that the Properties are set at Design time.

Changing the Properties

In this program we shall give the Form a title, ensure that the scrollbar has a range between 0 and 100 in steps of 1 and only one radio button appears to be active at any time.

The following changes to the Properties of the controls are made:

Form1 – **Text** to *Scrollbar multiplier*

4 Changing Properties

Label1 – **Text** to *Input*

Label2 – **Text** to *Output*

HScrollBar1 – **Min** to *0*, **Max** to *100*, **SmallChange** to *1*

GroupBox1 – **Text** to *Multiplier*

RadioButton1 – **Text** to *10*, **Checked** to *True*

RadioButton2 – **Text** to *20*, **Checked** to *False*

RadioButton3 – **Text** to *50*, **Checked** to *False*

When you have completed the Property changes, the Form should have the appearance shown in Figure 4.2 with the x10 multiplier button with a dot in it.

We must now add the code.

Adding the Code

We shall add this in sections according to the controls. In the previous chapter you were shown how to access each section of code as required so it may be a good time to check that out if you need reminding how to do it.

The RadioButtons

This adds the multiplier to the code

```
Private Sub RadioButton1_CheckedChanged(ByVal sender As
System.Object, ByVal e As System.EventArgs) Handles
RadioButton1.CheckedChanged

    'Multiply by 10
    mult = 10

End Sub
```

Remember the first and last lines do not have to be typed in.

```
Private Sub RadioButton2_CheckedChanged(ByVal sender As Object,
ByVal e As System.EventArgs) Handles
RadioButton2.CheckedChanged
```

```
'Multiply by 20
mult = 20

End Sub
```

```
Private Sub RadioButton3_CheckedChanged(ByVal sender As Object,
ByVal e As System.EventArgs) Handles
RadioButton3.CheckedChanged

    'Multiply by 50
    mult = 50
End Sub
```

Form Load

This line ensures that mult has a value allocated to it as a precaution in case any Radio button does not have a *Checked* property set to True when the Form is loaded.

```
Private Sub Form1_Load(ByVal sender As Object, ByVal e As
System.EventArgs) Handles MyBase.Load

    'Initialise Multiplier to 10
    mult = 10

End Sub
```

Scroll bar

Whenever the scroll bar is moved, calculations take place which have to be transferred to the input and output boxes

```
Private Sub HScrollBar1_Scroll(ByVal sender As System.Object, ByVal
e As System.Windows.Forms.ScrollEventArgs) Handles
HScrollBar1.Scroll

    'Place scroll bar value into Textbox
    TextBox1.Text = HScrollBar1.Value
    'Perform multiplier action
    TextBox2.Text = HScrollBar1.Value * mult

End Sub
```

4 Changing Properties

Declaration

One variable *mult* has to be declared and this is inserted into General Declarations at the top of the code. You will notice that before this line is inserted an error message appears in the Task List at the bottom of the screen.

```
Public Class Form1
  Inherits System.Windows.Forms.Form

  'Declare mult as integer variable
  Private mult As Integer
```

Running the Program

Once the code has been inserted you can run the program. Remember the code is being saved automatically.

You should now get your Form appearing as in Figure 4.3.

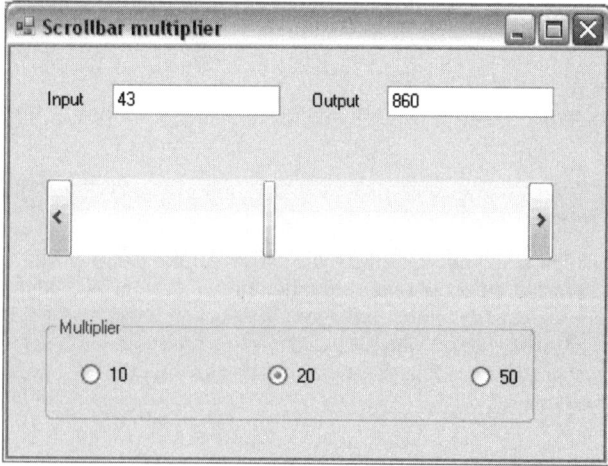

Figure 4.3 The Scrollbar multiplier program running

As the scroll bar is moved you will see the numbers in the input and output boxes change. Check that they give the correct answers.

Exercises

The following two exercises will give you an opportunity to try out your Visual Basic 2005 Express skills. You have already encountered all of the controls and it is a case of laying out the Forms as shown and then inserting the appropriate code.

Exercise 4.1

The Form in Figure 4.4 will enable you to calculate the volume of a rectangular tank. Insert the dimensions in boxes A, B and C and the volume will be calculated when the Calculate button is clicked.

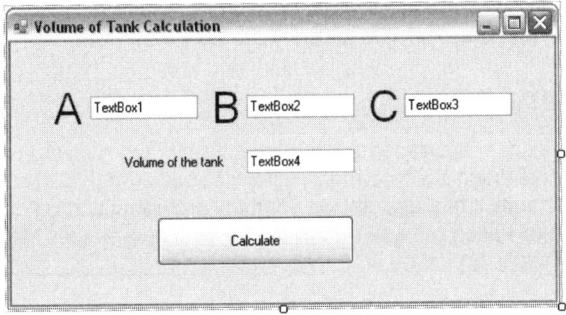

Figure 4.4 Volume of rectangular tank Form

Exercise 4.2

This Form (Figure 4.5) is a temperature converter; Fahrenheit to Celsius (DegF to DegC) and Celsius to Fahrenheit (DegC to DegF). The temperatures are set by the scroll bars and each time they are moved, the temperature is calculated.

The conversion between Celsius (C) and Fahrenheit (F) is:

$$C = (F-32) \times 5/9$$

4 Changing Properties

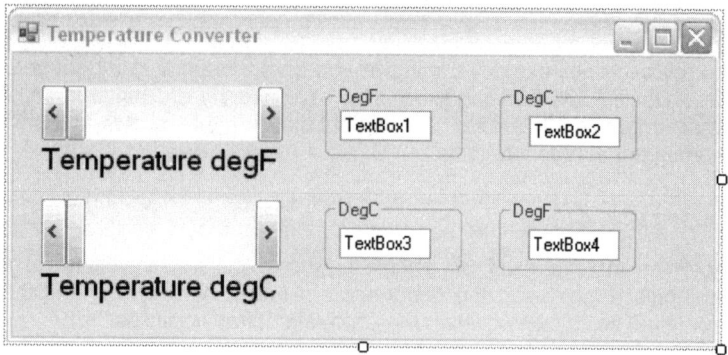

Figure 4.5 The temperature converter Form

Summary

This chapter has introduced some new controls and shown you how to alter the Properties so that the program behaves in a particular way. Most importantly it has also shown you how programs can be developed with only a few lines of code and at the same time are user friendly and are also visually appealing.

We now need to learn a bit more about the mechanics of Visual Basic 2005 Express programs before using our controls in some more demanding programs.

5
A Loop and Timer

The programs that we have created so far have been very interactive and required the click of a button in order to get a response. An important feature of a computer is that it can be used for automation, which means that once it has been started it will then carry out a series of operations before stopping. How can this be done in Visual Basic 2005 Express?

It really requires the program to create a chain of events which are followed until one event signals the end of the process. This can be done with something which is called a loop and there are several different types that are available to us in Visual Basic 2005 Express. The one that we shall consider here is a For... Next loop. Others we shall consider in later chapters are Do...While loops and Case structures. They all have their place and we shall use them when appropriate.

Another control we shall introduce in this chapter will be the Timer which is extremely important in any type of automation process. The Timer enables us to control the rate of a process and this can be very fast or extremely slow. The choice is ours.

Whereas the loop and timer will be important aspects of this chapter, three other features will be introduced. Two of these will enhance the Form and make it appear very much more professional. These are the menu bar and the scrollbars within textboxes. The menu bar is an alternative to buttons and the scrollbars enable hidden text in a textbox to be revealed. They are easy to use and make the Form more intuitive in its use. The third is a mathematical function which creates random numbers. This is an ideal source of data which we can manipulate in many different ways, or we can use it to create dice games or a lottery.

As you can gather there is plenty to learn in this chapter. So let us get started on the first of the two projects that we shall study by starting up Visual Basic 2005 Express and creating a New Project called Example 5.1.

5 A Loop and Timer

Example 5.1

This program will generate 100 random numbers and display them in a textbox. It will then be possible to clear the textbox before generating a further 100 numbers and the operation can be repeated as often as required.

First of all put a Textbox on the Form (Figure 5.1).

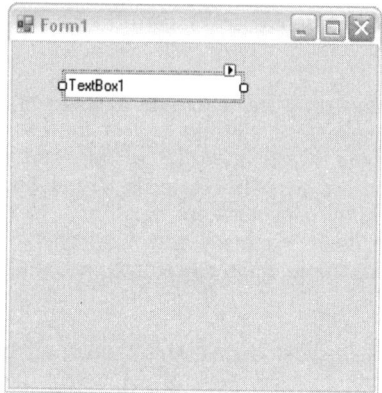

Figure 5.1 Textbox on Form

Now select a MenuStrip object from the Toolbox (Figure 5.2).

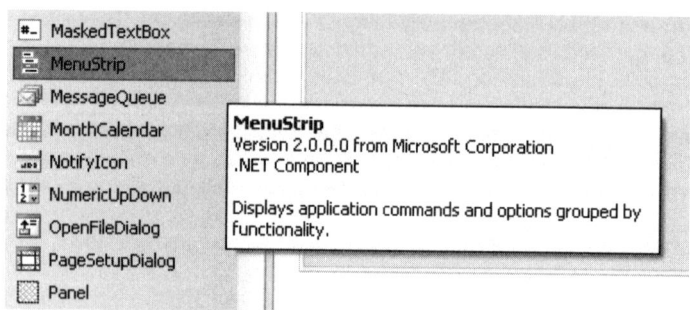

Figure 5.2 The MenuStrip control

The MenuStrip object will locate itself between Textbox1 and the Form1 Text. Immediately a box appears within this space with the words *Type*

A Loop and Timer 5

Here in it and MenuStrip1 appears in a window beneath the Form window (Figure 5.3).

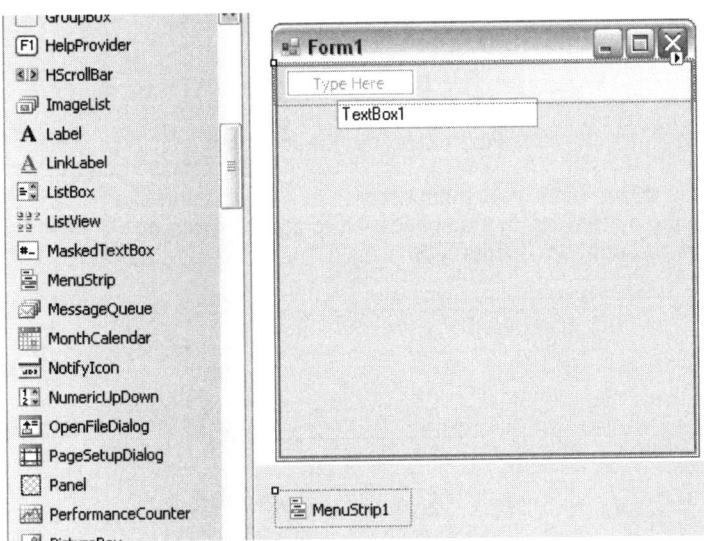

Figure 5.3 MenuMenu1

Where it states *Type Here*, type in *Generate*. As you click on the box and start to type two further Type Here boxes appear (Figure 5.4).

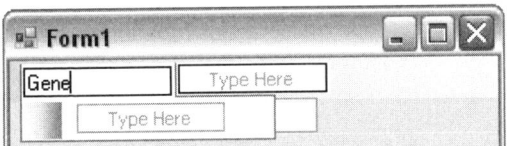

Figure 5.4 The creation of menu bar boxes

The boxes below and to the right of the one we are using to indicate where further menu bar objects may be typed. Once *Generate* has been inserted, the Form has the appearance shown in Figure 5.5.

53

5   A Loop and Timer

Figure 5.5 The new menu bar

There is one more object that we wish to place in the menu bar and this is done by clicking on the space next to the Generate box. A new *Type Here* box appears (Figure 5.6)

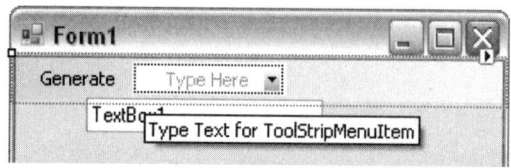

Figure 5.6 An additional menu bar box

We can now type in *Exit* into the box which will complete the Form after changing the Form Text to *Random Numbers* (Figure 5.7).

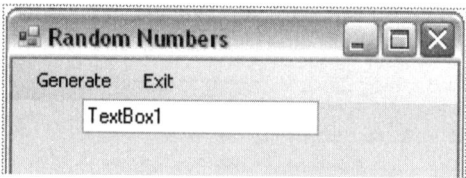

Figure 5.7 The completed Form

We must now insert the code.

The Code

The flow chart in Figure 5.8 illustrates how the program will work.

A Loop and Timer 5

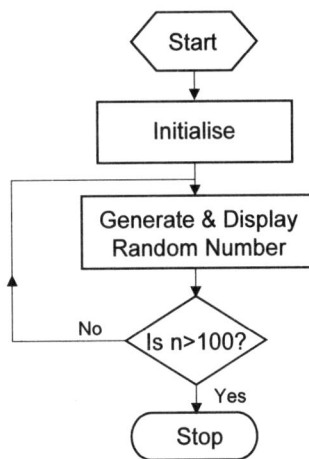

Figure 5.8 The random numbers flow chart

The process consists of a loop in which 100 random numbers are generated and displayed in a text box. There are several ways of presenting the numbers but the method selected here is to string the numbers together separated by commas. This is a process called concatenation and you will see how this in done in the code shown below. It does require some preparation for the character string variable that is going to be used. This is initially made a null variable in this particular case.

The Generate menu bar box

Double-click on the Generate menu bar box and insert the following code into the Sub MenuItem1_Click routine.

```
Private Sub GenerateToolStripMenuItem_Click(ByVal sender As System.Object, ByVal e As System.EventArgs) Handles GenerateToolStripMenuItem.Click

'Declare the variables
    Dim n As Integer
    Dim A As String
    Dim B$ = ""
    'Reseed random number generator
```

5 A Loop and Timer

```
    Randomize()
    'For...Next loop
    For n = 1 To 100
        'Store random number
        A = Int(Rnd(1) * 100)
        'Add random number to character string
        B$ = B$ + A + ","
        'Display character string
        TextBox1.Text = B$
        Next

End Sub
```

Let us now look more closely at the code.

Initially we declare the variables which we wish to use. As they are only to be used in this sub-routine we do not have to make them Public. The variable n is the loop counter value and A is the integer variable which will contain the random number after it has been multiplied by 100. B$ is a character string which will contain the concatenated random numbers and commas so that we initialise it by making it a null string.

Visual Basic 2005 Express has a random number generator but like many software generated random numbers they can duplicate the same numbers each time. This is overcome by using *Randomize* which enables fresh sets of random numbers to be generated by a process of seeding the PC's system clock. It works very well as will soon be seen.

The For...Next loop enables the 100 random numbers to be generated. Each random number is between 0 and 1 and so if we multiply by 100 and then use Int(), we shall get integer random numbers between 0 and 100. These numbers are then concatenated into a long string which is displayed in the text box each time the loop is processed.

The Exit menu bar box

The code is completed by double-clicking on the Exit box and inserting the following code into the MenuItem 2 sub-routine.

```
Private Sub ExitToolStripMenuItem_Click (ByVal sender As System.Object, ByVal e As System.EventArgs) Handles ExitToolStripMenuItem.Click
```

A Loop and Timer 5

```
'End Project
    End

End Sub
```

This sub-routine has just the statement *End* in it which will terminate the program.

Running the Program

The program is now complete and Figure 5.9 show what happens when it first runs.

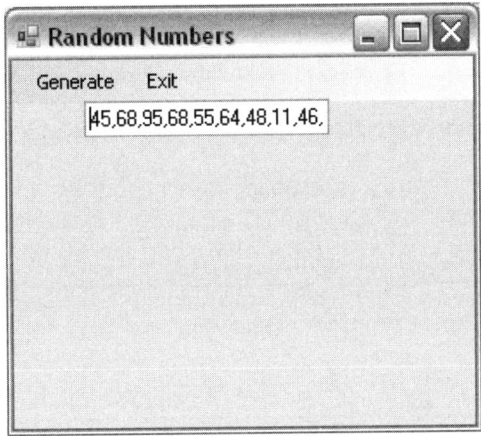

Figure 5.9 Capturing 100 random numbers

It can be seen that the textbox is too small. It can be made larger by changing the Multiline property of TextBox to True (Figure 5.10).

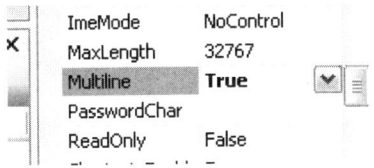

Figure 5.10 Changing the Multiline property

57

5 A Loop and Timer

This affects the Textbox as shown in Figure 5.11.

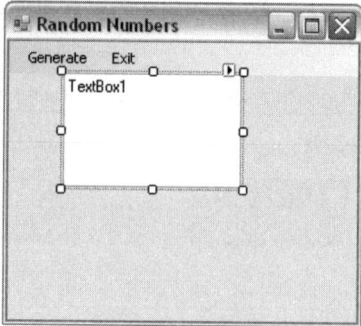

Figure 5.11 A Multiline Textbox

The numbers are now displayed better (Figure 5.12).

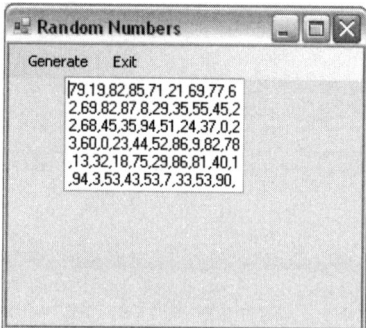

Figure 5.12 The Multiline display of numbers

There are times when the textbox is restricted in space so that it cannot be increased in size. Under these circumstances a scroll bar is the solution. This is easily done by highlighting the Textbox and then going to ScrollBars in the Property window (Figure 5.13).

A Loop and Timer 5

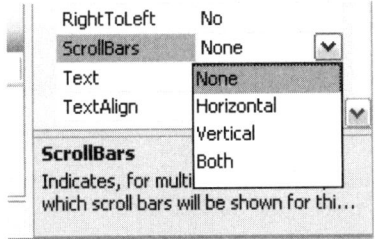

Figure 5.13 Textbox scroll bars

The choice is now up to you. In this case Vertical scroll bars seem most appropriate and Figure 5.14 shows them in use.

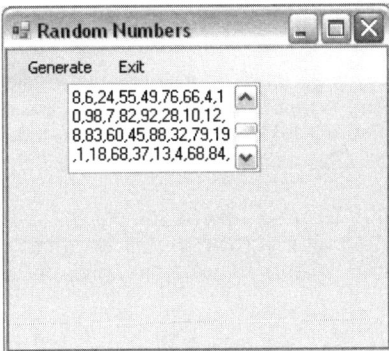

Figure 5.14 Using vertical scrollbars

We can now scroll up and down and see all the numbers that have been generated.

Exercise 5.1

Modify the code so that only one number per line is generated.

Exercise 5.2

Remove the *Int* of the random number and narrow the text box so that only part of the number is displayed. Add the horizontal scrollbar so that you can view all of the numbers by scrolling.

5 A Loop and Timer

Example 5.2

You will have noticed that the random numbers in Example 5.1 appeared very quickly. There are times when a slower rate of display may be useful and this can be achieved using the Timer object. With the Timer it is possible to control rates from any time from one thousandth of a second upwards and this creates some excellent programming opportunities with Visual Basic 2005 Express.

What we will do is to take the program in Example 5.1 and add a timer and counter box on to the Form. It will then be a case of rearranging our code. As the Form and code have similarities to our new requirements we shall start off with a copy of Example 5.1 and adjust it accordingly.

Making a copy of Example 5.1 Project

This has to be done outside the Visual Basic 2005 Express environment. Starting with **Start>My Computer**, locate the folder that contains the Example 5.1 folder. Perform a Copy and Paste to obtain a Copy of Example 5.1. Rename this folder Example 5.2.

In Visual Basic 2005 Express open Example 5.2 using Open Project. You will be confronted with an Example 5.1 file which you should open. The Solution Explorer window will have the appearance shown in Figure 5.15.

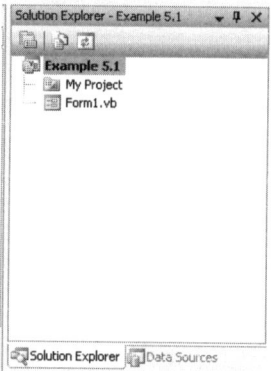

Figure 5.15 Solution Explorer for Example 5.2

A Loop and Timer   5

Several *'Example 5.1'*s need to be changed.

With the solution file it is a case of changing *Example 5.1* to *Example 5.2* in the Solution Explorer file (Figure 5.16).

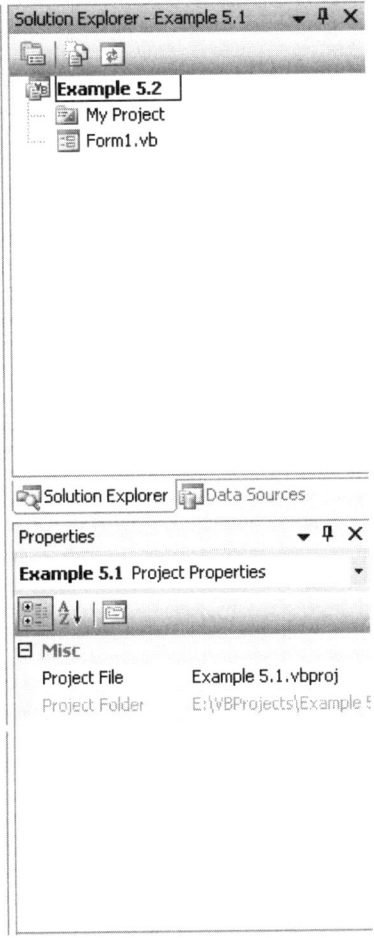

Figure 5.16 Changing the name of the Solution file

The other 5.1s now change to 5.2 automatically (Figure 5.17).

5 A Loop and Timer

Figure 5.17 The Example 5.2 changes are appearing

There is one problem and that is the IDE heading which still shows *Example 5.1* (Figure 5.18).

A Loop and Timer   5

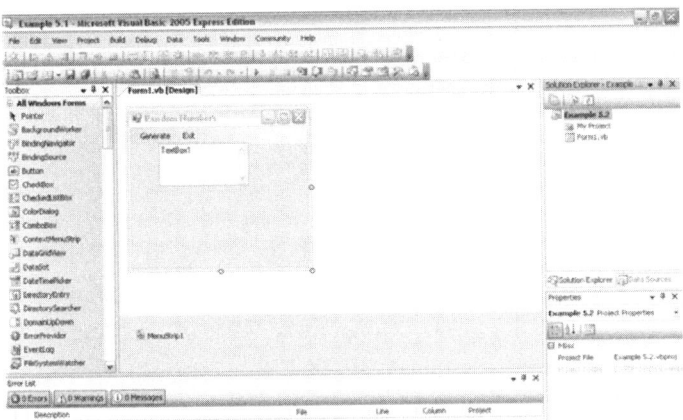

Figure 5.18 The current state of Example 5.2 IDE

When the project is closed, we return to the Example 5.2 folder (Figure 5.19).

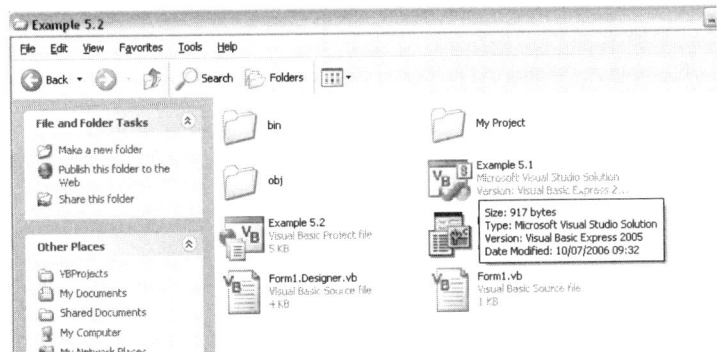

Figure 5.19 Example 5.2 folder

The Example 5.1 file needs to be renamed to Example 5.2. You will now see all files are designated as Example 5.2 in this folder (Figure 5.20).

5 A Loop and Timer

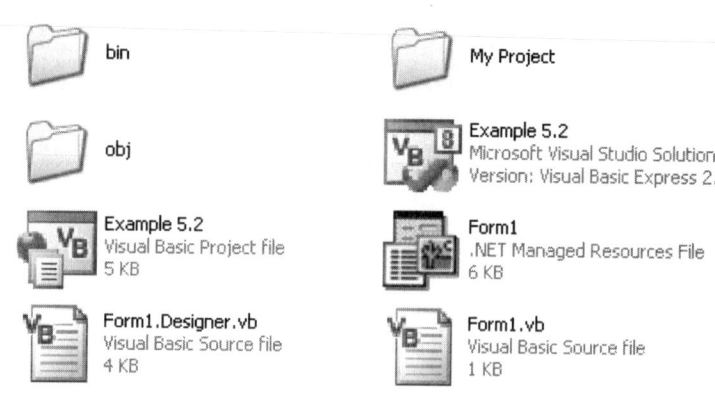

Figure 5.20 The updated Example 5.2 folder

In summary the following steps are required to copy a file:

1. Make a copy of selected file
2. Paste it in the appropriate folder and rename it
3. Load it into Visual Basic 2005 Express
4. Rename the Solution Explorer file
5. Close the project in Visual Basic 2005 Express.
6. Return to the new project folder and rename file which still possesses the original file name.
7. Check that the new project loads into Visual Basic 2005 Express.

Creating Example 5.2

Load Example 5.2 into Visual Basic 2005. A second textbox is now added to the Form and when the Timer is transferred from the ToolBox to the Form it immediately appears in the window below the Form Window that already contains MenuStrip1 (Figure 5.21). The File Name is changed to *Random Numbers - timed*.

A Loop and Timer 5

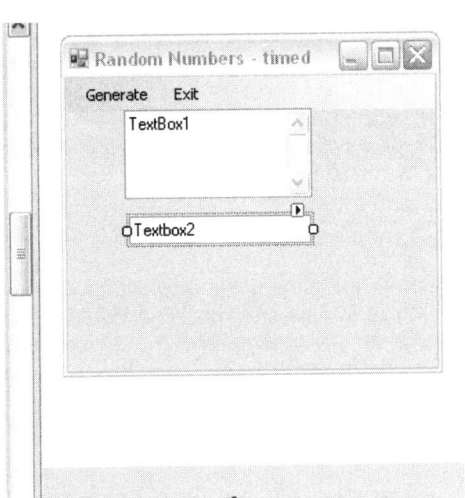

Figure 5.21 The Example 5.2 Form

It is worthwhile considering the properties of Timer1. Figure 5.22 shows the default settings with the Interval set to *100ms* and Enabled set to *False*.

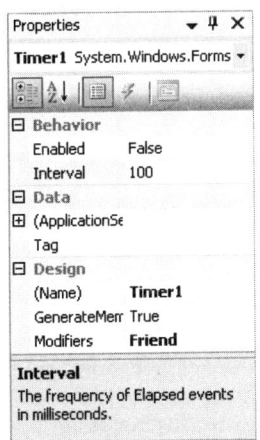

Figure 5.22 The Timer 1 properties

5   A Loop and Timer

These default settings mean that Enabled must be made True before the timer operates at 100ms intervals.

Hardly any alterations have taken place with the Form but the code will need a great deal of consideration.

The Code

Instead of 100 random numbers being displayed we shall have only 10 and each appearing at 100ms intervals. The For...Next loop has been replaced by the Timer sub-routine and the Generate sub-routine is reduced to some simple statements. One important feature is that variable parameters are used in separate sub-routines and as a consequence they are moved to the top of the program so that their values can be public.

We shall consider each part of the program in turn.

The Generate ToolStrip MenuItem

This is the Generate sub-routine.

```
   Private Sub GenerateToolStripMenuItem_Click(ByVal sender As System.Object, ByVal e As System.EventArgs) Handles GeneToolStripMenuItem.Click

'Reseed random number generator
    Randomize()
    'Clear textbox
    TextBox1.Text = ""
    'Clear character string
    B$ = ""
    'Enable Timer
    Timer1.Enabled = True

End Sub
```

In Example 5.1 we had the actual acquisition of 100 random numbers, in this example the Generate sub-routine re-seeds the random number generator and clears the two textboxes. In addition it starts the clock and it is in the timer sub-routine where all the action is.

The Exit ToolStrip MenuItem

This sub-routine remains unchanged from that in Example 5.1.

```
Private Sub ExitToolStripMenuItem_Click(ByVal sender As System.Object, ByVal e As System.EventArgs) Handles ExitToolStripMenuItem.Click

   'End Project
   End

End Sub
```

Timer1

The timer sub-routine is called at 100ms regular intervals so that it may be regarded as a timed loop. To keep track of the number of times it is activated we use a count variable n, which is incremented each time the sub-routine is used. This number is also displayed on the Form.

The random number is generated, concatenated into a string and displayed in a similar way to how it was done in Example 5.1.

The number of counts is checked using an *If...End If* statement and when 10 counts have been completed, the counter is switched off and the generation of new random numbers ceases.

```
   Private Sub Timer1_Tick(ByVal sender As Object, ByVal e As System.EventArgs) Handles Timer1.Tick

   'Increment counter
   n = n + 1
   'Display counter
   TextBox2.Text = n
   'store random number
      A = Int(Rnd(1) * 100)
      'Add random number to character string
      B$ = B$ + A + ","
      'Display character string
   TextBox1.Text = B$
   'Check counter
   If n > 9 Then
      'Disable counter
      Timer1.Enabled = False
      n = 0
```

5 A Loop and Timer

```
    End If
  End Sub
```

Declarations

As this program is using a repetitive sub-routine we do not want to keep on declaring the variables and especially the character string B$. The most sensible thing is to move them to the top of the code where they also become Public.

```
Public Class Form1
  'Declare variables
  Dim n As Integer
  Dim A As String
  Dim B$ = ""
```

Running Example 5.2

In the case of Example 5.1 we had 100 random numbers appearing in the textbox almost instantaneously. With Example 5.2 we have only 10 but they appear at a much slower pace so that you can actually see the counter increment (Figure 5.23).

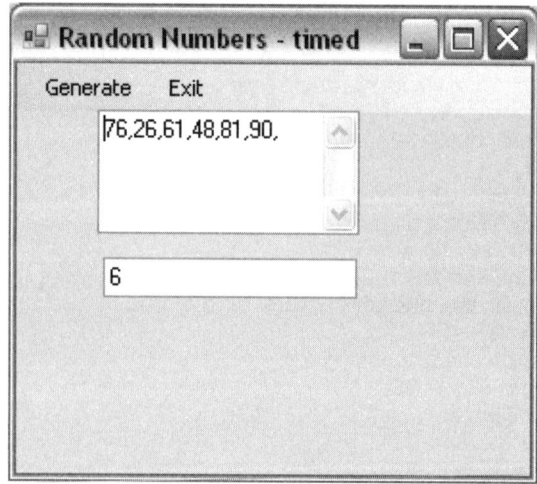

Figure 5.23 The timed random number generator

Summary

You may have limited application of random numbers but this chapter has introduced some interesting examples of applications of Visual Basic 2005 Express. Example 5.1 showed how the For...Next loop can be used and how a Menu bar can be placed on a Form. We then showed how a complete project can be re-used in a new project by copying and renaming a folder. Then in Example 5.2 we saw how a timer can be used and also how a program that has been used in a previous application can be re-formed to accommodate different looping processing.

Knowing how to time and loop are important Visual Basic 2005 Express skills and we shall return to them on numerous occasions in the future.

5 A Loop and Timer

6
Picture Boxes

This chapter is devoted to placing images on the Visual Basic.NET Form. Images can be added to the Form using an object called a Picture Box and this provides some control over the positioning and size of the image on the Form. Images come in many formats and Visual Basic.NET can import the following:

- i) Bitmap – the file extension is .bmp
- ii) Icon – the file extension is .ico
- iii) Metafile – a Microsoft Windows metafile has the file extension .wmf
- iv) GIF – the file extension is .gif
- v) JPEG – the file extension is .jpg

These files can be generated by any application which supports the particular format and Paintshop Pro, Adobe Photoshop, etc., are popular packages for this task.

Images can be added at Design time or Run time. In an earlier chapter it has been explained that Design time is the period in which the project is been prepared whilst Run time is when the project is actually working.

Images

There are a wide range of pictures that can be considered to be images. Nowadays it is very easy to obtain pictures from digital cameras, download pictures from the internet or obtain clipart pictures from software packages that are used every day. In the examples used in this chapter we shall use bitmaps and icons which can be found in the Program Files. Within these folders there are several types of images. These include:

Bitmaps, Icons, Cursors, Metafiles and Video

It is a useful exercise to go to these folders via **Start>My Computer** and see what types of images are available. The one thing you may discover is that some images are very big and in some way they need to be shrunk down to a size which we can place on a Form. The safest

6   Picture Boxes

images to use are icons which are made up of 16 x 16 pixels or 32 x 32 pixels. A pixel is the smallest unit in which a monitor screen can be divided. A typical monitor screen has a size of 1024 x 768. These icons will be very small but Picture Boxes have a few tricks to make them larger.

Let us move on to display some images in a Picture Box. First of all we shall look at Design time images before looking at Run time situations.

Example 6.1

In the first of our examples we shall create a Form containing a Picture Box which will display two different size images according to which of two buttons is clicked.

Start up Visual Basic 2005 Express and create a New Project called Example 6.1.

Place a Picture Box and two Buttons on the Form as shown in Figure 6.1.

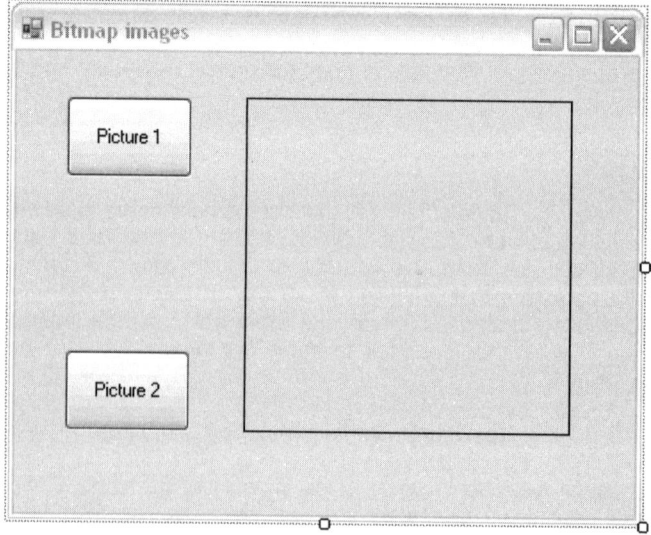

Figure 6.1 Example 6.1 Form

Picture Boxes 6

The Text properties for the Form and the two Buttons are changed as shown in Table 6.1:

Object	Text
Form	Bitmap images
Button 1	Picture 1
Button 2	Picture 2

Table 6.1 Changes in Text properties

Place a frame around the picture box by selecting FixedSingle out of the BorderStyle property (Figure 6.2).

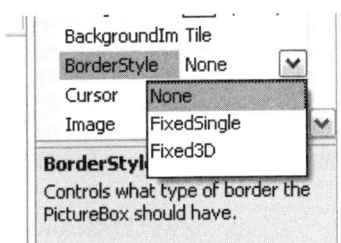

Figure 6.2 Selecting the Picture box surround

The Code

The code required for this program is very simple. The images reside in the *Microsoft MSDN 2005 Express Edition – ENU* folder of *Microsoft Visual Studio 8*. The full path is:

Program Files\Microsoft Visual Studio 8\Microsoft MSDN 2005 Express Edition – ENU

As you can see, this path is horrendously long and it is a good idea to copy the two bitmap images into a more accessible location. G:\VBProjects has been chosen in this example and the two files are logo.bmp and msdn.bmp.

One image is assigned to Button1 and the other to Button2. The code for the buttons is as follows:

6 Picture Boxes

Button1

```
Private Sub Button1_Click(ByVal sender As System.Object, ByVal e As System.EventArgs) Handles Button1.Click

    'Load 501 x 427 bitmap image
    PictureBox1.Image = Image.FromFile("E:\VBProjects\logo.bmp")

End Sub
```

Button2

```
Private Sub Button2_Click(ByVal sender As System.Object, ByVal e As System.EventArgs) Handles Button2.Click

    'Load 110 x 60 bitmap image
    PictureBox1.Image = Image.FromFile("E:\VBProjects\msdn.bmp")

End Sub
```

In each case the same code is used for PictureBox1 and you may see why it is prudent to move the images to a folder with a relatively short path.

The code required to put the image into the Picture box is far from intuitive and the question has to be asked where such code examples can be found. The simple answer is the Microsoft MSDN library which can be accessed from **Help>Search** provided the library has been loaded with Visual Basic 2005 Express, or alternatively it can be obtained from the Microsoft website at http://msdn1.microsoft.com/en-gb/default.aspx .

Running the Program

No more code has to be added so we can just run it as it is. It is then a question of simply either clicking the left button for Picture 1 or the right one for Picture 2. Figures 6.3 and 6.4 show the results.

Picture Boxes   **6**

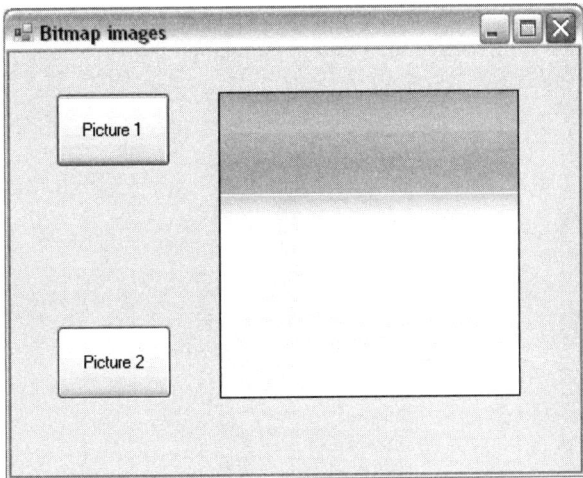

Figure 6.3 Picture 1

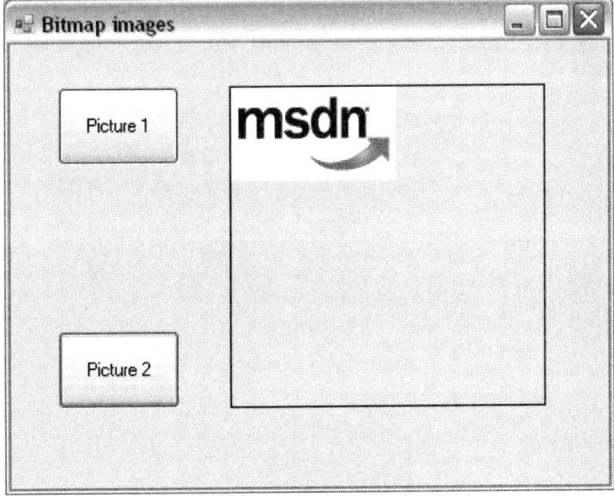

Figure 6.4 Picture 2

6 Picture Boxes

You will notice that the image of Picture 2 does not fill the Picture box frame. To ensure that it does you must change the SizeMode property to AutoSize (Figure 6.5).

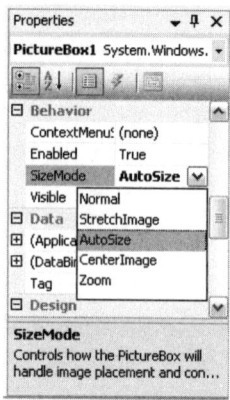

Figure 6.5 Selecting AutoSize

Re-run Example 6.1 and you will find that you will get a very much larger image for Picture 1 (Figure 6.6) and a complete image for Picture 2 (Figure 6.7).

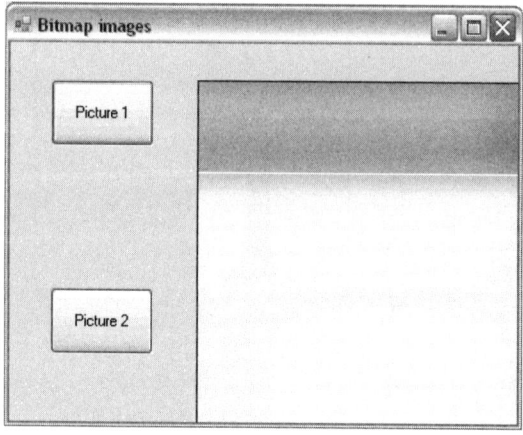

Figure 6.6 The complete Picture 1

Picture Boxes 6

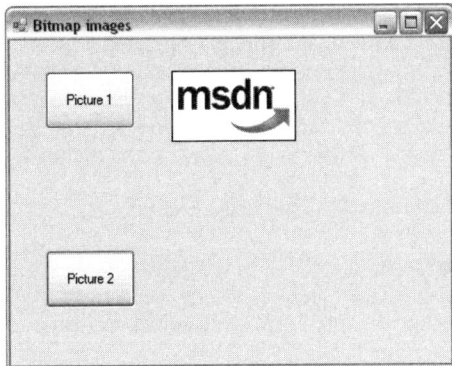

Figure 6.7 Picture2 without any excess frame

If we return to picture 1, it is possible to make the Form larger by stretching the Form. This will enable the whole of the image to be shown as in Figure 6.8.

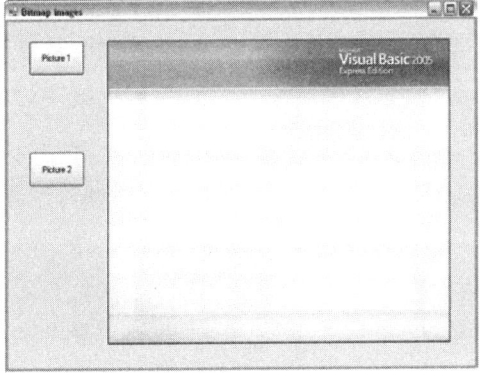

Figure 6.8 The complete image displayed

You have seen that we can alternately replace one picture by another in a picture box. The Example also illustrates how larger bitmap images are. The next stage is to do the process in such a way that the picture appears to move. In other words we can create animation.

6 Picture Boxes

Animation

In animation one frame of an image is replaced by another in which there is a slight change in position of certain parts of the original image. Use enough images and you can create a film but remember that a cinema film runs at 25 frames per second so that a 1 minute film contains 1500 images. Anyway how do we make a start?

First of all start a new project and call it Example 6.2.

Example 6.2

Place a PictureBox on the Form and select the properties shown in Table 6.2

Property	Setting
BorderStyle	FixedSingle
Size	76,76

Table 6.2 PictureBox1 properties

Use Copy and Paste of PictureBox1 to create PictureBox2 and PictureBox3. Align the three Picture boxes as shown in Figure 6.9.

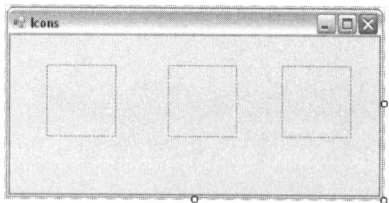

Figure 6.9 The three Picture boxes

Exercise 6.1

Use the Layout Toolbar (Figure 6.10) to align the three boxes.

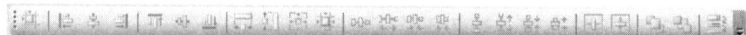

Figure 6.10 The Layout Toolbar

Adding the Images

This example is going to load the images at Design time so that we will be investigating how this is achieved. Returning to PictureBox1 we need to add the image, therefore click on PictureBox1 and select Image in the Properties window (Figure 6.11).

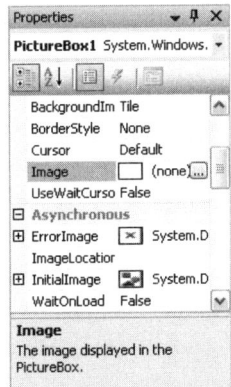

Figure 6.11 The Image property

Double-click on the three ellipses to the right of (none) and bring up the Select Resource window (Figure 6.12).

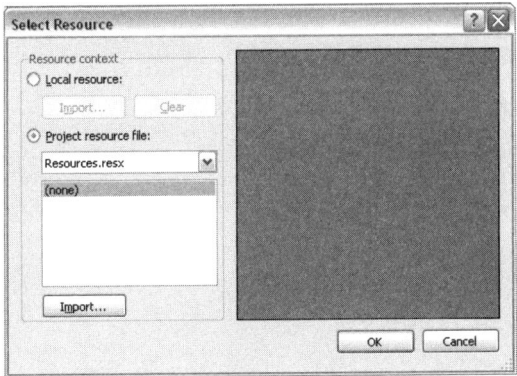

Figure 6.12 The Select Resource window

6 Picture Boxes

Click on *Import* and navigate from Program Files to Forms in the Microsoft Office folder. Select the 1033 folder and obtain the various images shown in Figure 6.13.

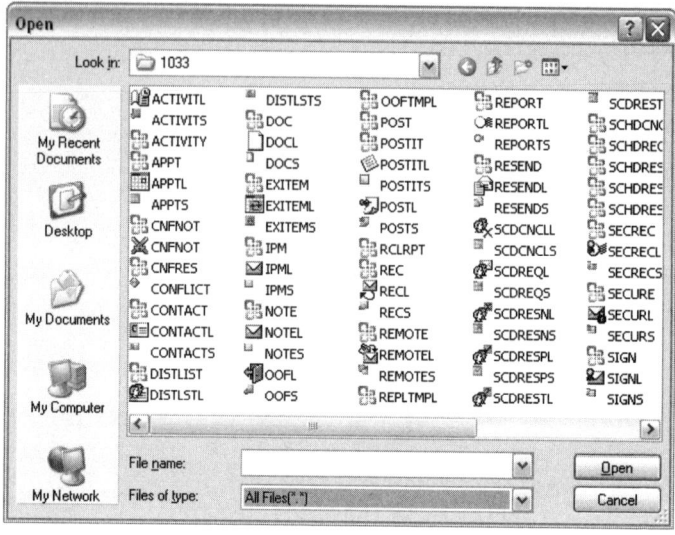

Figure 6.13 The 1033 Open window

Double-click on *SCDRESNL* and obtain the image in PictureBox1 (Figure 6.14).

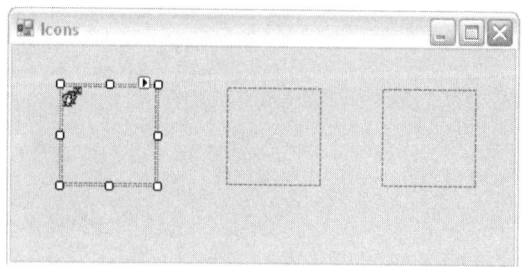

Figure 6.14 SCDRESNL in PictureBox1

Picture Boxes 6

The image is too small for the Picture box. If you look again at Figure 6.11 you will see that the Tip box aligned to the file SCDRESNL shows that the size of the image is 32 x 32 bits. We need larger images to fill the space.

Fortunately there is a StretchImage property available to picture boxes (Figure 6.15) and when this is selected the image fills the frame (Figure 6.16).

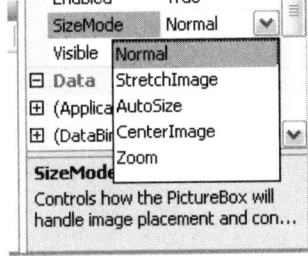

Figure 6.15 Selecting the StretchImage SizeMode

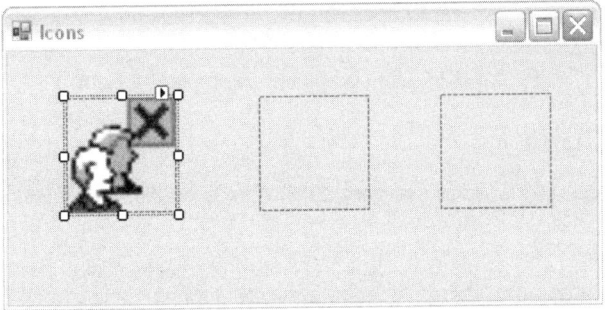

Figure 6.16 The stretched image

Be careful not to select the AutoSize StretchMode as this will only shrink the Picture box frame to the original image size. The major shortcoming of the stretched image is that the various lines become more ragged as the image is increased in size.

6 Picture Boxes

Exercise 6.2

Repeat the process of putting images into PictureBox2 and PictureBox3. *SCDRESPL* is placed in PictureBox2 and *SCRESNL* in PictureBox3. The Visible property of both these Picture boxes should be made *False*.

Change the Text of the Form to *Icons*.

The Example 6.2 Form should now look like Figure 6.17.

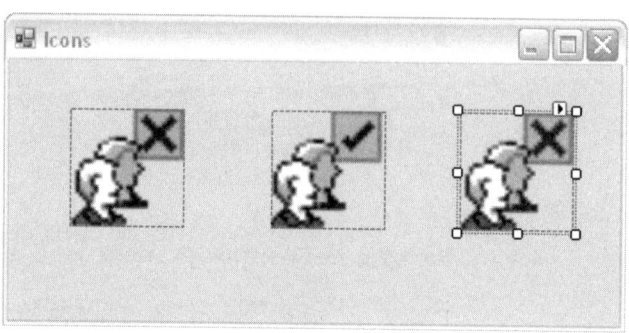

Figure 6.17 The completed Example 6.2 Form

The Code

The code that is added is very short and is confined to PictureBox1. Double-click on PictureBox1 to bring up the Code Window and add the following code.

```
Private Sub PictureBox1_Click(ByVal sender As System.Object, By
Val e As System.EventArgs) Handles PictureBox1.Click

If PictureBox1.Image Is PictureBox2.Image Then
     PictureBox1.Image = PictureBox3.Image
  Else
     PictureBox1.Image = PictureBox2.Image
  End If

End Sub
```

Each time PictureBox1 is clicked the status of the image is checked. If PictureBox2 image is present it is replaced by that of PictureBox3 and vice versa. What should happen is that the images should change each time PictureBox1 is clicked.

Placing SCDRESNL in PictureBox1 to start with ensures that we are not confronted with an empty frame when the program is started up.

Running Example 6.2

When you run the program you should get a cross box and a tick box appearing alternately each time you click the picture box (Figure 6.18 and Figure 6.19).

Figure 6.18 Incorrect icon

Figure 6.19 Correct Icon

Note that the PictureBox2 and PictureBox3 are hidden when the program is running. Example 6.3 takes this process further.

6 Picture Boxes

Example 6.3

The light sequence of traffic lights is a good example of something that changes at a regular rate and images of traffic lights can be used in an animation setup. Example 6.3 shows this can be done using Group boxes containing picture boxes. Group boxes can be hidden or made visible along with any of its contents and this example demonstrates this very well. It also shows that picture boxes can be used to display colour rather than images.

Traffic Lights

Traffic lights vary from one country to another but basically red means stop and green is go. The use of the amber or yellow light is quite vague. In this example we shall use the sequence of:

> Red
> Red + Amber
> Green
> Amber
> Red

You can adjust the sequence to your requirements later and add a pedestrian crossing if you wish.

The Form

Create a project called Example 6.3 and set out a Group box containing three Picture boxes and a Button as shown in Figure 6.20.

Figure 6.20 Example 6.3 Form

Picture Boxes 6

The *Text* of the Group box is changed to *Red* and the BackColor of each Picture box is changed by using the BackColor in the Property window and selecting the Custom option (Figure 6.21).

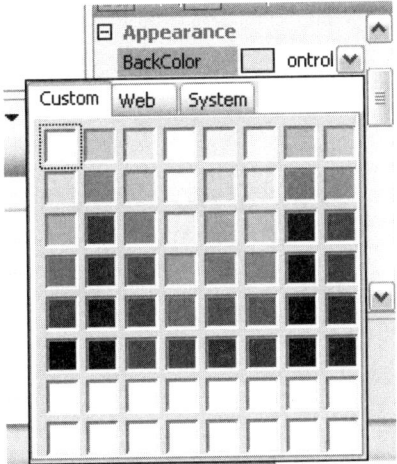

Figure 6.21 Selecting the BackColor

The BackColor of Picturebox1 is made Red and those of the other two Picture boxes are made Black so that the Form takes on the appearance shown in Figure 6.22.

Figure 6.22 The completed Red traffic light

6 Picture Boxes

Use copy and paste to duplicate the Group boxes three times and change the Form Text to Traffic Lights. Also alter the BackColors of the Picture boxes to the appropriate colors along with Texts of the Group boxes. Your Form should then look similar to the one in Figure 6.23.

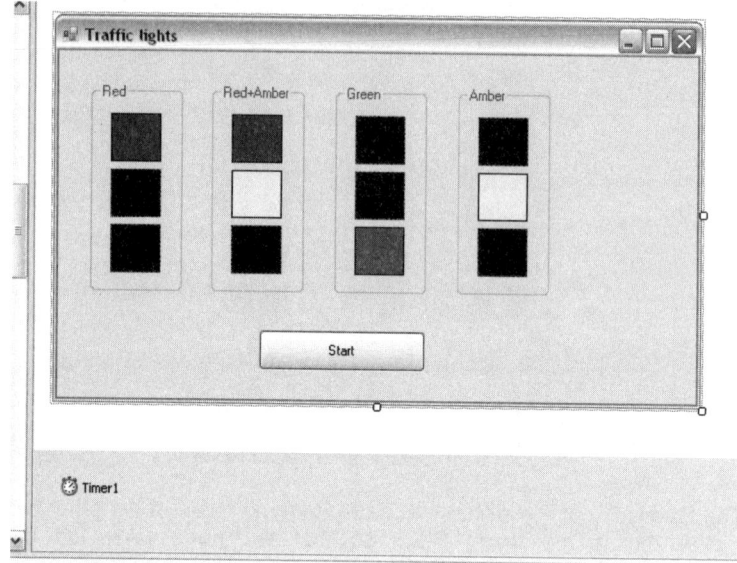

Figure 6.23 The completed Traffic lights Form

The Visible properties of Group boxes 2, 3 and 4 are made False. A timer is also added with an Interval property of 500.

The Code

The code for this example is a little more complicated than the previous two examples. Let us take each part at a time.

Button1

Button1 is a dual-purpose button. When the Start button is clicked the text will change to Stop and the timer will be enabled. When the Stop button is pressed the Start text will return and the timer will be disabled.

Picture Boxes 6

```
Private Sub Button1_Click(ByVal sender As System.Object, ByVal
e As System.EventArgs) Handles Button1.Click

    'Check button status
    If Button1.Text = "Start" Then
        'Change button text
        Button1.Text = "Stop"
        'Switch on clock
        Timer1.Enabled = True
    Else
        'Change button text
        Button1.Text = "Start"
        'Switch clock off
        Timer1.Enabled = False
    End If

End Sub
```

Timer1

Each time this sub-routine is activated a different Group box will appear. The appropriate way of doing this process is to use a Select Case structure. This is done by having a number of Cases which are activated when a certain condition is satisfied. In this particular situation the Case is selected by the state of a counter which is incremented each time the Timer sub-routine is activated. Within each Case one image is switched off and another is switched on. In the final Case of the structure the images are changed and the counter is reset so that the first Case is selected next time the timer sub-routine is called.

```
Private Sub Timer1_Tick(ByVal sender As System.Object, ByVal e
As System.EventArgs) Handles Timer1.Tick

    'Increment counter
    n = n + 1
    'Change traffic light setting
    Select Case n

        Case 1
            'Red on, Amber on
            GroupBox1.Visible = False
            GroupBox2.Visible = True
```

6 Picture Boxes

```
      Case 2
        'Red off,Amber off, Green on
        GroupBox2.Visible = False
        GroupBox3.Visible = True
      Case 3
        'Green off, Amber on
        GroupBox3.Visible = False
        GroupBox4.Visible = True
      Case 4
        'Amber off, Red on
        GroupBox4.Visible = False
        GroupBox1.Visible = True
        'Zero counter
        n = 0
    End Select

End Sub
```

The traffic light achieved by this code is: Red+Amber, Green, Amber, Red. This process is then repeated.

Form Load

In the Form Load sub-routine the counter is initialised and the timer is switched off.

```
Private Sub Form1_Load(ByVal sender As Object, ByVal e
As System.EventArgs) Handles Me.Load

    'Initialise counter
    n = 0
    'Switch off clock
    Timer1.Enabled = False

End Sub
```

Declaration

The only declaration is to declare the counter variable which is used in the timer sub-routine.

Picture Boxes 6

```
Public Class Form1
    Dim n As Integer
```

Exercise 6.3

Can you predict what will happen when this program is run?

Running Example 6.3

When the program is run, the red traffic light will appear (Figure 6.24).

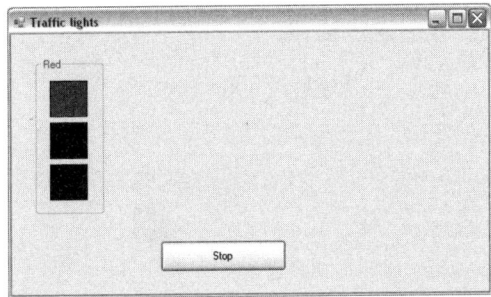

Figure 6.24 The initial state of the Traffic light program

When the Start button is clicked, the program will take over and the different traffic light Group boxes will become visible one at a time. The sequence is Red, Red + Amber, Green, Amber and then it will repeat indefinitely. This is illustrated in Figure 6.25.

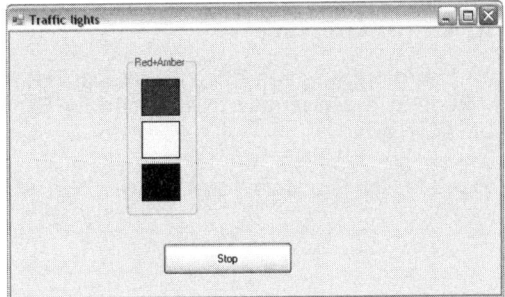

Figure 6.25a Red + Amber

6 Picture Boxes

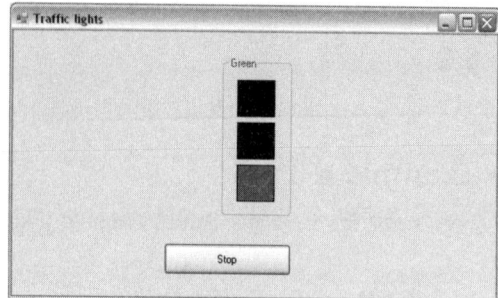

Figure 6.25b Green

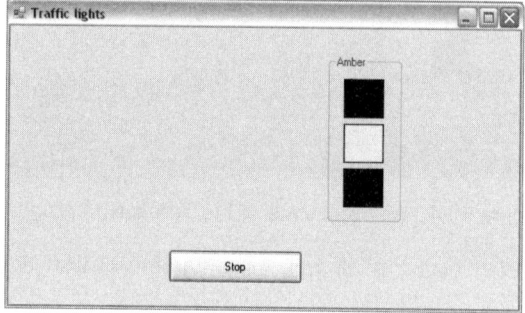

Figure 6.25c Amber

Improving Example 6.3

The rapid moving across the screen is too distracting. The alternative is to lay out the Form in a similar way to the Form for Example 6.2 or adopt a different approach.

It is possible to overlay the Group boxes as shown in Figure 6.26.

Picture Boxes 6

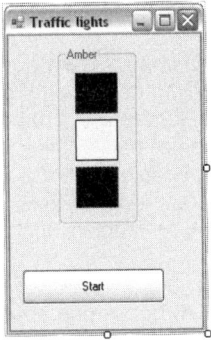

Figure 6.26 Overlay of the Group boxes

The order of the Group boxes is not too important as they are either visible or hidden. The advantage of this method is that the Form becomes very compact and easier to manage.

You can check that it works and the order is not important by trying different arrangement of the overlays. You should get the results shown in Figure 6.27 when the program is running.

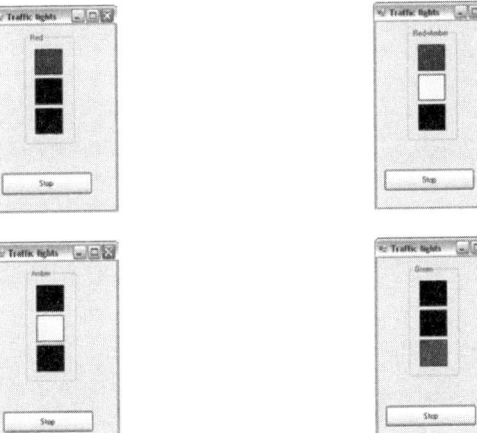

Figure 6.27 The traffic lights working in a clockwise sequence

6 Picture Boxes

Summary

This chapter has shown how images can be placed on a Form using the Picture Boxes. We have looked at loading the image at run-time and at design-time. The major problem with the run-time application is that the path of the image is an integral part of the program. This means that a program may not be very portable especially if it is on a flash memory drive which acquires different drive letters depending upon the PC which is being used. This is a problem that needs care and attention when it is used.

Using images with the picture box is one application of its use. Another application is with colour as used in the Traffic lights program. Picture boxes do have other applications and the next chapter shows how Picture boxes can be used to plot graphs, which opens up another interesting topic.

7
Graphs

Graphs are pictorial representations of data. They reveal a great deal of information about data as they illustrate trends and any abnormalities in the data. From a graph it is relatively easy to determine whether the source of data is working correctly and if new data needs to be collected. Graphs are a powerful indicator as to whether or not the data is good or bad. The human eye is considered to be the most powerful instrument in detecting any fault and by representing it in the form of a picture, i.e. a graph, data can be initially analysed almost at a glance. From then on any mathematical analysis can be performed with a certain degree of increased confidence.

Visual Basic 2005 Express does not have a graphing object though earlier versions of Visual Basic did have MSChart which had some shortcomings. Fortunately this does give us the opportunity to devise alternative methods and the Picture box is ideal for the purpose. This chapter will deal with plotting data in graphical form and Chapter 9 will look at how bar and pie charts can be created.

The Picture box

We encountered the Picture box in the previous chapter and showed how it can be used to display images. This is the primary purpose of the Picture box but it can be used equally well for the drawing of graphs.

A Picture box can be considered to be a sheet of graph paper upon which the vertical and horizontal axes of a graph are drawn. The lengths of the axes depend upon the values of the data being plotted and the scale that has to be selected. Sometimes this may mean that a graph is small and occupies a small area, on other occasions it can be very large. We have to have a very good understanding of the scales we are using.

The Pixel

The scale used in the Picture box is the pixel. A pixel is a *pic*ture *el*ement where *pic* is replaced by *pix*. The pixel is defined as the smallest element of a picture and can be considered in the same way as the 1mm squares that are found in mm graph paper. The one advantage of a Picture box is that it can be stretched in the vertical and

7 Graphs

horizontal directions to make it larger (provided you do not exceed the size of the screen) – one thing you cannot do with graph paper!

The Graph

The graphs we shall plot in this chapter are Cartesian graphs. This means that the horizontal and vertical axes increase linearly from the origin at the bottom left-hand corner (Figure 7.1).

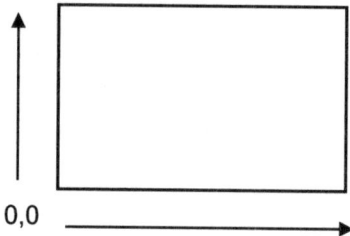

Figure 7.1 The Cartesian graph system

Each point of the graph that is plotted has a horizontal and vertical property which is called a co-ordinate. Normally the horizontal co-ordinate value is designated as an x value and the vertical one as a y value. The origin therefore has the co-ordinates (0, 0) as seen in Figure 7.1.

The Scale

We now know that the unit used in a Picture box is the pixel but we should also be aware that the origin of the scale is the top left-hand corner of the picture box. This means that the origin of the co-ordinate system for the Picture box is at the top left-hand corner (Figure 7.2).

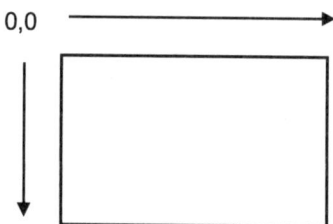

Figure 7.2 The Picture box coordinate system

This means that care has to be taken when plotting points on this system. The easiest way of learning how scales and axes are drawn on Picture boxes is to actually experiment and that is what we shall initially do. First of all we do need to know how to draw a line on a Picture box.

Line drawing

Drawing a line in a Picture box is a simple task provided you follow some simple rules. As explained in Chapter 6 the Picture box has a host of applications available to it which must be defined before use. MSDN Help is again a powerful source of information.

Initially we have to tell the Picture box that it is going to be used for graphs and this is done in the following statement:

```
Dim g As Graphics = PictureBox1.CreateGraphics
```

This means that the variable g will be used in the program to indicate Picture box graphics.

The next statement defines the device which will perform the drawing and this is a pen in this case. The pen has to have a colour which is defined below.

```
Dim pen1 As New Pen(Color.Black)
```

Having put the above statements in the Declarations we can now draw a line.

```
g.DrawLine(pen1, x1,y1,x2,y2)
```

This statement draws a black line from x1,y1 to x2,y2. If the distance between the two co-ordinate points is made small, a smoother graph will result. Therefore it is important to ensure that a sufficient number of points are used so that a smooth plot is obtained.

We now have the basic facts on drawing lines in a Picture box. Let us apply them to drawing the frame of a graph which will be a grid. We shall develop it stage by stage so that each part fits together and you can change values to see what happens.

7 Graphs

Example 7.1

Example 7.1 will develop drawing a grid in easy steps. Create a new project and call it Example 7.1. Change the Text of the Form to *Graph Axes* and place a PictureBox on the Form. Using MenuStrip add two ToolStripMenuItems with the names of *Generate* and *Exit* (Figure 7.3).

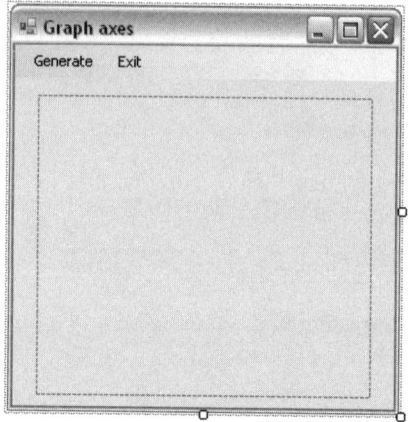

Figure 7.3 The Example 7.1 Form

The Code

The code will be contained in the Generate ToolStripMenuItem but we must not forget the Exit ToolStripMenuItem which will have its code added first of all.

Exit ToolStripMenuItem

This will terminate the program and is the same code as we have encountered several times before.

```
Private Sub ExitToolStripMenuItem_Click(ByVal sender
As System.Object, ByVal e As System.EventArgs)
Handles ExitToolStripMenuItem.Click

    'End Program
    End

End Sub
```

Generate ToolStripMenItem

This part of the program will develop so that we shall introduce new statements, run the program and review the results.

```
Private Sub GenerateToolStripMenuItem_Click(ByVal sender As
System.Object, ByVal e As System.EventArgs)
 Handles GenerateToolStripMenuItem.Click

    'Declare graph variables
    Dim g As Graphics = PictureBox1.CreateGraphics
    Dim pen1 As New Pen(Color.Black)

    'Draw graph frame
    g.DrawLine(pen1, 0, 0, 250, 0)

End Sub
```

The three statements in this code are the ones that were introduced earlier. Let us now run the program. Figure 7.4 shows the result.

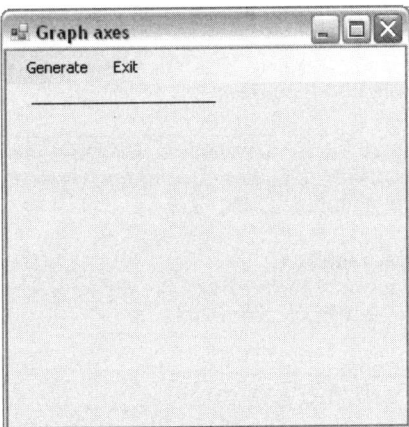

Figure 7.4 Drawing the first line

We have drawn a horizontal line from (0, 0) to (250, 0). This line is supposed to be 250 pixels long, but is it? To make sure let us increase the size of the Picture box and re-run the program (Figure 7.5).

7 Graphs

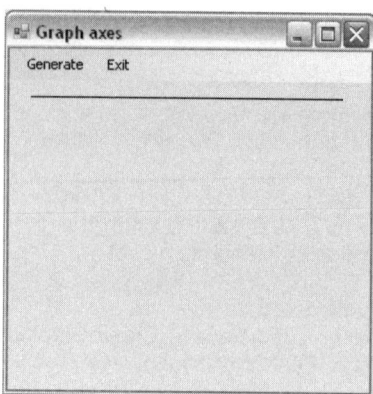

Figure 7.5 Re-drawing the line

The line is longer yet we have not re-written the code. We have increased the size of the PictureBox to ensure that the whole line is produced. This is something with which we have to be very careful. Make sure the Picture box is large enough to accommodate the graph. It is better too have it too large to start with and then shrink it to a more suitable size once the program has been fully completed.

Let us now add a vertical line. The statement is in **bold italics** and ToolStripMenuItem1 now becomes:

```
Private Sub GenerateToolStripMenuItem_Click(ByVal sender As
System.Object, ByVal e As System.EventArgs) Handles
GenerateToolStripMenuItem.Click

    'Declare graph variables
    Dim g As Graphics = PictureBox1.CreateG raphics
    Dim pen1 As New Pen(Color.Black)

    'Draw graph frame
    g.DrawLine(pen1, 0, 0, 250, 0)

    g.DrawLine(pen1, 0, 200, 0, 0)

End Sub
```

Graphs 7

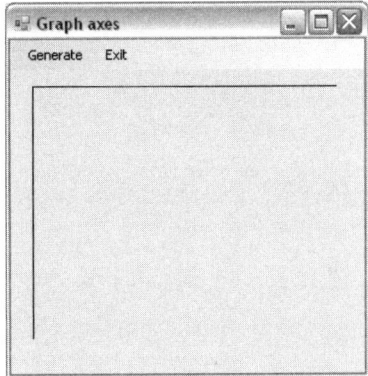

Figure 7.6 Adding the vertical line

The line goes 200 pixels vertically downwards. If you think that is too short and part of it is missing, increase the size of the picture box.

Let us now complete the rectangle by adding another horizontal and vertical line. Again the lines to be added are in ***bold italics***.

```
Private Sub GenerateToolStripMenuItem_Click(ByVal sender As
System.Object, ByVal e As System.EventArgs) Handles
GenerateToolStripMenuItem.Click

   'Declare graph variables
   Dim g As Graphics = PictureBox1.CreateGraphics
   Dim pen1 As New Pen(Color.Black)

   'Draw graph frame
   g.DrawLine(pen1, 0, 0, 250, 0)
   g.DrawLine(pen1, 250, 0, 250, 200)
   g.DrawLine(pen1, 250, 200, 0, 200)

   g.DrawLine(pen1, 250, 0, 250, 200)
   g.DrawLine(pen1, 250, 200, 0, 200)

   g.DrawLine(pen1, 0, 200, 0, 0)

End Sub
```

7 Graphs

This completes the rectangle of side 200 x 250 pixels. Figure 7.7 shows what you get when you run the program.

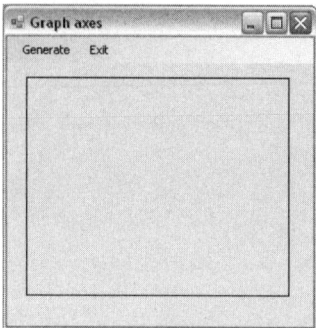

Figure 7.7 The completed rectangle

Again if any sides are missing, increase the size of the Picture box.

When you draw a graph on a piece of paper you first of all draw the axes and then you mark off the scales on both axes. This is our next task to mark off the axes with the little marks called tick markers. These occur at regular intervals and can be created with For...Next loops. It will also require two variables to be declared and this can be seen in the code below. The code to be added is again shown in ***bold italics***.

```
Private Sub GenerateToolStripMenuItem_Click(ByVal sender As
System.Object, ByVal e As System.EventArgs) Handles
GenerateToolStripMenuItem.Click

  'Declare graph variables
  Dim g As Graphics = PictureBox1.CreateGraphics
  Dim pen1 As New Pen(Color.Black)

  Dim n As Integer
  Dim j As Integer

  'Draw graph frame
  g.DrawLine(pen1, 0, 0, 250, 0)
  g.DrawLine(pen1, 250, 0, 250, 200)
  g.DrawLine(pen1, 250, 200, 0, 200)
  g.DrawLine(pen1, 0, 200, 0, 0)
```

```
'Horizontal tick markers
For n = 1 To 9
  j = n * 25
  g.DrawLine(pen1, j, 200, j, 190)
Next
'Vertical tick markers
For n = 1 To 9
  j = n * 20
  g.DrawLine(pen1, 0, j, 10, j)
Next
End Sub
```

Let us run the program before we analyse it (Figure 7.8).

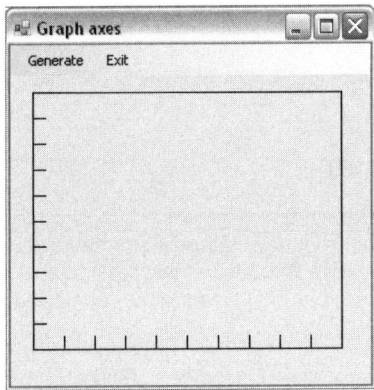

Figure 7.8 The axes with tick markers

Each of the tick markers has a length of 10 pixels. The vertical ones are spaced at intervals of 20 pixels, the horizontal ones at 25. The g.Drawline statement is quite different for the vertical and horizontal cases. In the vertical case we draw from (j,0) to (j,10) whilst in the horizontal case it is (200,j) to (190,j). Cast your mind back to where we stated that the co-ordinate (0, 0) is for the Picture box. This is the reason for using the value of x = 200 as the baseline.

Exercise 7.1

Modify the values used in drawing the horizontal and vertical tick markers so that a proper grid is drawn (Figure 7.9).

7   Graphs

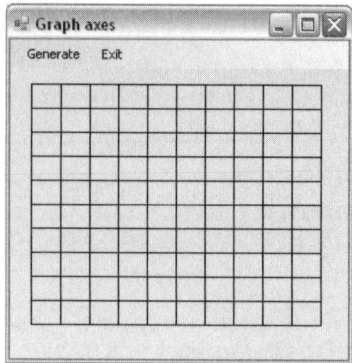

Figure 7.9 The graph grid

Having drawn the grid, let us now plot some graphs.

The Sine Wave

The most straightforward graph to plot is a sine wave which is shown in Figure 7.10. The two important features are the amplitude, i.e. how high or low it swings above or below the horizontal zero axis, and the frequency, i.e. the number of cycles that are completed in 1 second.

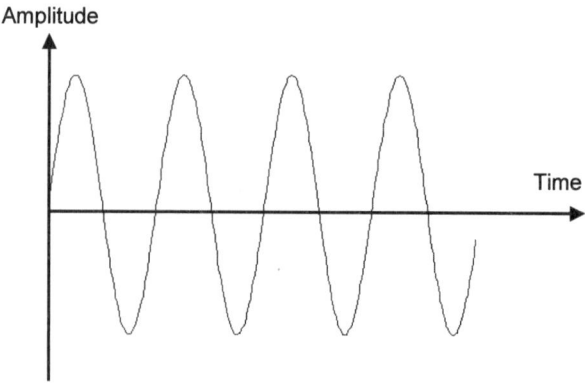

Figure 7.10 Sine wave drawn as a function a time

The amplitude and the frequency will be two important features of the program that we will develop.

The equation of a sine wave is y=A sin(2πft) where A is amplitude, f is the frequency, y is the displacement in the vertical direction and t is the time which is in the horizontal direction.

In Visual Basic 2005 Express the sine wave is in a Math Class and is expressed as:

Math.Sin()

This is the expression that we shall use in the next example, Example 7.2.

Example 7.2

We shall use Example 7.1 as the basis of this new example so it is a case of copying and pasting the Example 7.1 and renaming the folder and all relevant parts as Example 7.2. Change the Form Text to *Sine Wave Graph*.

ToolStripMenItem1 requires the following code which only requires slight modifications to what we had before. Again additions are in ***bold italics***.

```
Private Sub GenerateToolStripMenuItem_Click(ByVal sender As System.Object, ByVal e As System.EventArgs) Handles GenerateToolStripMenuItem.Click

    'Declare graph variables
    Dim g As Graphics = PictureBox1.CreateGraphics
    Dim pen1 As New Pen(Color.Black)

    Dim pen2 As New Pen(Color.Green)

    Dim n As Integer
    Dim j As Integer

    Dim y1 As Integer
    Dim y As Integer
```

7   Graphs

```
'Draw graph frame
g.DrawLine(pen1, 0, 0, 250, 0)
g.DrawLine(pen1, 250, 0, 250, 200)
g.DrawLine(pen1, 250, 200, 0, 200)
g.DrawLine(pen1, 0, 200, 0, 0)
'Horizontal tick markers
For n = 1 To 9
   j = n * 25
   g.DrawLine(pen1, j, 200, j, 0)
Next
'Vertical tick markers
For n = 1 To 9
   j = n * 20
   g.DrawLine(pen1, 0, j, 250, j)
Next
'Load first point data
y1 = 100

'Plot random number data
For n = 0 To 250
   'Load sine wave data
   y = 100 - 100 * Math.Sin(2 * 3.142 * n / 250)
   'Plot points
   g.DrawLine(pen2, (n - 1), y1, n, y)
   'Store current data value
   y1 = y
Next
End Sub
```

In the Declaration section we have introduced a new pen which will enable data to be plotted in a different colour. There are also two new variables which are required to plot the graph.

Once the grid has been plotted we can consider how to plot the sine wave. The vertical axis of the graph is 200 pixels and this will be the peak to peak swing of the sine wave. Therefore the maximum amplitude that we can use is 100 pixels. The start position of the sine wave must be half way up the vertical axis which means that we will have an offset of 100. This explains the value of y1 and the 100s which appear in the sine wave equation.

Graphs 7

y1 is a reference value which will be continually reset to the previous calculated value of the sine wave so that the line can be drawn from the previous position to the current position.

The argument in the Math.Sine brackets represents 2πft. 'ft' in this case is n/250 where n is the variable from 0 to 250. This ratio ensures that one complete cycle of a sine wave is generated. This is verified when the program is run (Figure 7.11).

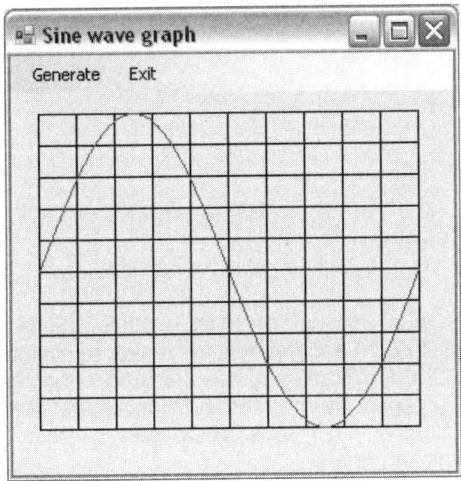

Figure 7.11 The sine wave graph

The next stage in this development is to alter the amplitude and frequency. This can be done in Example 7.2 by changing the values in the equation in the program but a better method is shown in Example 7.3.

Example 7.3

Once again we do not want to lose the good work that we have done in Example 7.2 so we need to copy, paste and rename the folder, Example 7.3. Make other changes necessary so that the Solution and .vboroj are both Example 7.3.

7 Graphs

Modify the Form so that it has the appearance shown in Figure 7.12.

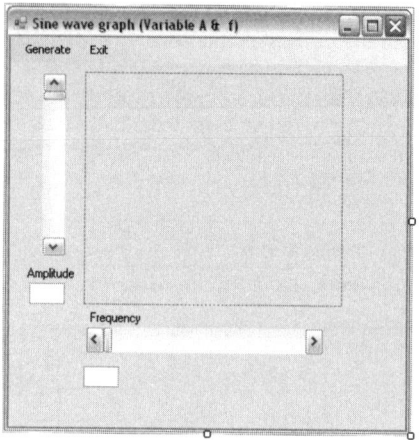

Figure 7.12 Variable A and f sine wave

The principal changes are the Form Text which is changed to *Sine wave graph (Variable A and f)* and the addition of two scroll bars. The vertical scroll bar alters the Amplitude and has Textbox1 associated with it. The Frequency is changed by the horizontal scroll bar and its value is displayed in Textbox2. The two labels identify the textbox values and also act as labels for the axes.

The Code

The code is more extensive than in Example 7.2 and this is mainly to accommodate the changes that occur as scrollbars are adjusted. The whole program is presented and it just needs careful checking to ensure that it is correct.

Generate TooStripMenuItem

```
Private Sub GenerateToolStripMenuItem_Click(ByVal sender As
System.Object, ByVal e As System.EventArgs)
Handles GenerateToolStripMenuItem.Click

   'Declare graph variables
   Dim g As Graphics = PictureBox1.CreateGraphics
```

```
Dim pen1 As New Pen(Color.Black)
Dim pen2 As New Pen(Color.Green)
Dim n As Integer
Dim j As Integer
Dim y1 As Integer
Dim y As Integer
Dim Amp As Integer
Dim Freq As Integer

'Clear graph
PictureBox1.Refresh()
'Draw graph frame
g.DrawLine(pen1, 0, 0, 250, 0)
g.DrawLine(pen1, 250, 0, 250, 200)
g.DrawLine(pen1, 250, 200, 0, 200)
g.DrawLine(pen1, 0, 200, 0, 0)

'Horizontal tick markers
For n = 1 To 9
   j = n * 25
   g.DrawLine(pen1, j, 200, j, 0)
Next
'Vertical tick markers
For n = 1 To 9
   j = n * 20
   g.DrawLine(pen1, 0, j, 250, j)
Next

'Load first point data
y1 = 100
'Load amplitude
Amp = VScrollBar1.Value
'Load frequency
Freq = HScrollBar1.Value

'Plot sine wave data
For n = 1 To 250
   'Load sine wave data
   y = 100 - Amp * Math.Sin(2 * 3.142 * n / Freq)
   'Plot points
   g.DrawLine(pen2, (n - 1), y1, n, y)
   'Store current data value
   y1 = y
Next
```

7 Graphs

```
End Sub
```

This sub-routine now includes statements to acquire Amplitude and frequency prior to actually plotting the graph. The PictureBox1.Refresh() clears the PictureBox before drawing the axes and plotting the graph.

Exit ToolStripMenuItem

```
Private Sub ExitToolStripMenuItem_Click(ByVal sender
As System.Object, ByVal e As System.EventArgs) Handles
ExitToolStripMenuItem.Click

    'End Program
    End

End Sub
```

The Scrollbars

These set the amplitude and frequency.

VScrollbar1

The VScrollBar1 sets the Amplitude and the Max and Min properties are set to 100 and 1 respectively. LargeChange is also set to 1. The value is displayed in Textbox1.

```
Private Sub VScrollBar1_Scroll(ByVal sender As System.Object,
ByVal e As System.Windows.Forms.ScrollEventArgs)
Handles VScrollBar1.Scroll

    ' Display amplitude
    TextBox1.Text = VScrollBar1.Value

End Sub
```

HScrollbar1

The HScrollBar1 sets the Frequency and the Max and Min properties are set to 250 and 10 respectively. LargeChange is again set to 1.

The value is converted into a pseudo frequency by taking the reciprocal of the scrollbar setting divided by 250. This is stating that 250 units are equivalent to 1 complete cycle and lower values of the scrollbar will produce greater number of cycles.

```
Private Sub HScrollBar1_Scroll(ByVal sender As System.Object,
ByVal e As System.Windows.Forms.ScrollEventArgs)
Handles HScrollBar1.Scroll

   'Display frequency
   TextBox2.Text = 1 / (HScrollBar1.Value / 250)

End Sub
```

Form Load

This section of code ensures that the two text boxes have the initial settings of the scrollbars displayed when the program is run.

```
Private Sub Form1_Load(ByVal sender As System.Object, ByVal e
   As System.EventArgs) Handles MyBase.Load

   ' Display amplitude
   TextBox1.Text = VScrollBar1.Value
   'Display frequency
   TextBox2.Text = 1 / (HScrollBar1.Value / 250)

End Sub
```

Running Example 7.3

This is a program that produces different results depending on the settings of the variables. Figure 7.13 shows a small amplitude with a high frequency.

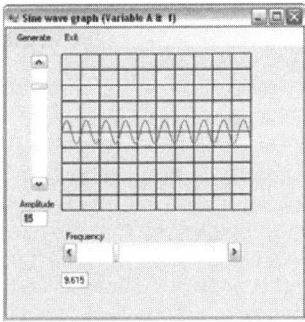

Figure 7.13 Small amplitude, high frequency sine wave

7 Graphs

Figure 7.14 shows a large amplitude with a lower frequency.

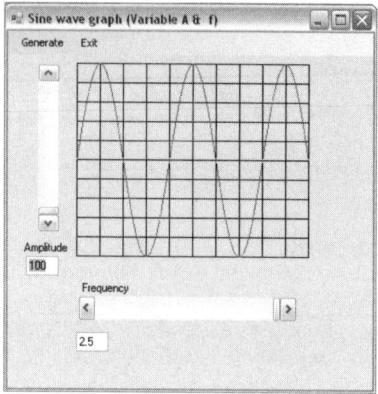

Figure 7.14 Large amplitude, lower frequency sine wave

Plotting Acquired Data

We now need to apply our knowledge of plotting graphs to data which is acquired at regular intervals of time. It is a case of using the *Timed random number generator* (Example 5.2) developed in Chapter 5 and plotting the results using the graphing process that we have developed in this chapter. This example is a test of what you have learnt already so that the minimum of explanation will be provided but to help you the details of the Form and Code are presented below. Your task is to write the program, test it and answer a few questions that are posed along the way.

The only new feature is:

Dim A(11) as integer

This is declaring the variable A as an array. We shall deal more with arrays in a later chapter but all you need to know for the present is that it is a method of storing numbers so that they can be accessed later. Each number is identified by the order in which it occurs in the series. In the case of our example here, 11 numbers will be stored and it is possible to choose any one of them at will, e.g. the third, the sixth, the ninth, etc.

Example 7.4

Start a new project and call it Example 7.4. Set up the following Form and Code and do the Exercises.

The Form

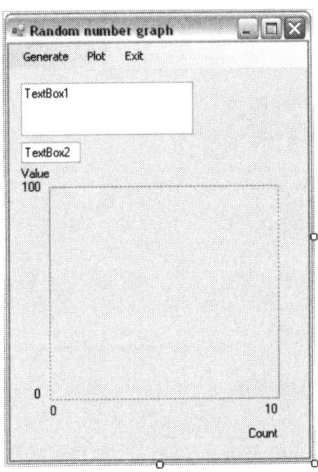

Figure 7.15 Example 7.4 Form

There are 3 ToolStripMenuItems, 2 Textboxes, 4 Labels, 1 PrintBox and 1 Timer on this Form.

Exercise 7.2

The 4 labels have their Visible property set to *False*. What happens when the program is run?

The Code

Declarations

```
Public Class Form1
'Declare the variables
Dim n As Integer
Dim A(11) As Integer
```

7 Graphs

```
Dim B$ = ""
```

Generate ToolStripMenItem

```
Private Sub GenerateToolStripMenuItem_Click(ByVal sender
As System.Object, ByVal e As System.EventArgs)
 Handles GenerateToolStripMenuItem.Click

    'Reseed random number generator
    Randomize()
    'Enable timer
    Timer1.Enabled = True
    'Clear textbox
    TextBox1.Text = ""
    'Clear character string
    B$ = ""
    n = 0

End Sub
```

Plot ToolStripMenuItem

```
Private Sub PlotToolStripMenuItem_Click(ByVal sender As
System.Object, ByVal e As System.EventArgs)
 Handles PlotToolStripMenuItem.Click

    'Declare graph variables
    Dim g As Graphics = PictureBox1.CreateGraphics
    Dim pen1 As New Pen(Color.Black)
    Dim pen2 As New Pen(Color.Green)
    Dim j As Integer
    Dim y1 As Integer
    Dim y As Integer

    'Clear graph
    PictureBox1.Refresh()
    'Draw graph frame
    g.DrawLine(pen1, 0, 0, 250, 0)
    g.DrawLine(pen1, 250, 0, 250, 200)
    g.DrawLine(pen1, 250, 200, 0, 200)
    g.DrawLine(pen1, 0, 200, 0, 0)

    'Horizontal tick markers
```

```
For n = 1 To 9
   j = n * 25
   g.DrawLine(pen1, j, 200, j, 0)
Next
'Vertical tick markers
For n = 1 To 9
   j = n * 20
   g.DrawLine(pen1, 0, j, 250, j)
Next

'Make scales visible
Label1.Visible = True
Label2.Visible = True
Label3.Visible = True
Label4.Visible = True

'Load first point data
y1 = 200 - 2 * A(0)

'Plot random number data
For n = 1 To 10
   'Load random number data
   y = 200 - 2 * A(n)
   'Plot points
   g.DrawLine(pen2, (n - 1) * 25, y1, n * 25, y)
   'Store current data value
   y1 = y
Next

End Sub
```

Exercise 7.3

What happens when the Labels are made visible?

MenuStrip

Code is required for three Menuitems.

Exit ToolStripMenuItem

```
Private Sub ExitToolStripMenuItem_Click(ByVal sender
As System.Object, ByVal e As System.EventArgs)
Handles ExitToolStripMenuItem.Click
```

7 Graphs

```
'End project
End

End Sub
```

Timer1

This is the code that makes the program actually work.

```
Private Sub Timer1_Tick(ByVal sender As System.Object, ByVal e
As System.EventArgs) Handles Timer1.Tick

    'Display counter
    TextBox2.Text = n
    'Store random number
    A(n) = Int(Rnd(1) * 100)
    'Add random number to character string
    B$ = B$ + Str$(A(n)) + ","
    'Display character string
    TextBox1.Text = B$
    'Increment counter
    n = n + 1
    'Check counter
    If n > 10 Then
        'Disable counter
        Timer1.Enabled = False
        n = 0
    End If

End Sub
```

Exercise 7.4

What does n >10 imply?

Form Load

This is the final piece of code to add.

```
Private Sub Form1_Load(ByVal sender As System.Object, ByVal e
As System.EventArgs) Handles MyBase.Load

    'Clear textboxes
    TextBox1.Text = ""
```

> TextBox2.Text = ""
>
> End Sub

Running Example 7.4

When Example 7.4 is run, a set of random numbers are displayed and plotted.

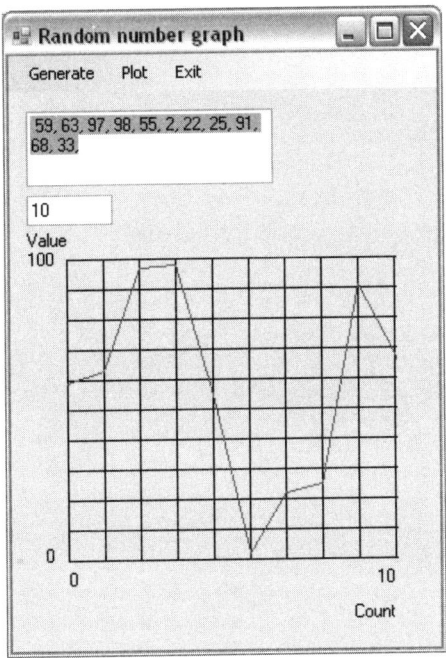

Figure 7.16 Data acquired with Example 7.4

Exercise 7.5

Do the random number data values agree with the plotted data?

Summary

This chapter has dealt with graphs. We have developed the method of plotting graph axes in the Picture box and shown how it is possible to

7 Graphs

plot mathematical equations. You have worked your way through a fairly long Visual Basic 2005 Express project and by now you should be reading and understanding how the program is being put together.

We are now in the position to look at more complex programs which actually start to interact with the PC itself. We know how to generate and plot data. We now need to know how to store it and recover it whenever we need it again. We need to look at data files in some detail.

8
Files

Data that we have produced in previous chapters has been lost as soon as we close down our Visual Basic 2005 Express programs. Sometimes we have felt that the data would be useful later but obviously we have no access to it. Fortunately we can save data whether it is numerical information, pictures or in alphanumeric form by storing on a hard disc drive, flash disc or even floppy discs. Each of these methods of data storage means that the information can be retrieved in the future.

We are accustomed to use Microsoft Office to store data, and Visual Basic 2005 Express which also comes from the Windows family can store information in a similar way. The important feature is that we have to go through certain processes to ensure that the data is stored in files in the appropriate format and that we do know how to recover the information. Normally if we store data in a particular way, we recover it in a similar way. There are some cases when this rule does not apply but for this chapter let us follow that method.

Data is stored in files and there is certain terminology used to describe the various processes that take place. It is important that we understand these terms, so there will be times in this chapter when a short explanation will be required before we can make any further progress.

This chapter will deal with three particular examples of data storage. In each case we shall deal with the storage and recovery of each type of data. In the first instance we shall consider a line of text, secondly we shall look a set of separate numbers and finally we shall look a continuous set of numbers separated by commas which is often referred to as a CSF, i.e. Comma Separated File, and is used by spreadsheet applications such as Microsoft Excel.

What are Files?

We have encountered files on many occasions as these are the things in which our Visual Basic 2005 Express projects have been saved. But what are they really? Well, data is stored in files in digital form. This means that data is stored as a series of *ones* and *zeroes*. This is the basis of the binary coding system which is the means by which pictures, numerical data and text are converted into digital form before storing.

8 Files

Sometimes in the case of pictures and some numerical data the information is already stored in binary form which means that little processing is required to store it. Other forms of numerical data and text have to be converted into digital form using a code which is called ASCII. ASCII stands for American Standard Code for Information Interchange. ASCII enables every key on the keyboard to be converted into binary form. The binary information can then be stored using the same method as data which was already in binary form.

Technically there are two processes that have to be programmed and we will concentrate on the storage of text based data. The storage of binary data (e.g. images) is a complicated process and beyond the scope of this book but will not be beyond your capabilities as your experience in Visual Basic 2005 Express becomes greater.

Preparing to store Data

You have become quite familiar now with typing a keyword into Visual Basic 2005 Express and it changing colour and type. When you add a point (i.e. a full-stop), a pop-up menu will then appear. This is reassuring as it gives you confidence that you are correctly typing in a program that will work. These keywords are often classes or controls and are a constituent part of Visual Basic 2005 Express. File and file management have their own classes and controls and they are activated using the System.IO Namespace which must be loaded before writing any programs dealing with files.

System.IO Namespace

Let us now add System.IO to a project. Start up Visual Basic 2005 Express and open a new project, e.g. Example 8.1.

Click on View Code for Form 1 and go the very top of the code, i.e. where the *Public Class Form1* statement is.

Go to the beginning of the statement and press the Enter key so that a line appears above the statement. Insert the line *Imports System.IO*. The top of the code shown now look like:

```
Imports System.IO

Public Class Form1
```

Files   8

The project will now handle the various File controls that we shall need.

Example 8.1

We could now describe all of the classes and controls that are involved in saving text to a file but the simplest way to do this is to look at a particular example and dissect the various parts.

The program is going to save some text to a file. We shall write some words in a textbox and then press a button to save the words. Therefore on the Example 8.1 Form place a textbox and a button. Change the text on the button to *Save* and that of the Form to *File writer* as shown in Figure 8.1.

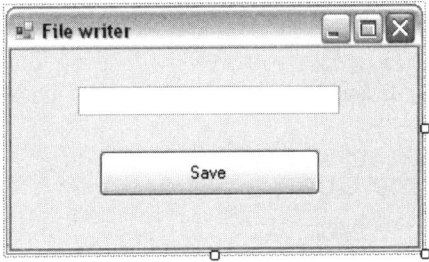

Figure 8.1 Example 8.1 Form

The Code

The code is only assigned to the button and is shown below:

```
Private Sub Button1_Click(ByVal sender As System.Object, ByVal e
As System.EventArgs) Handles Button1.Click

    'Declare filename variable
    Dim fname As String

    'Declare save file dialog
    Dim dlgSave As SaveFileDialog = New SaveFileDialog

    'Select save file dialog filter
    dlgSave.Filter = "Text Files|*.txt|All Files|*.*"
```

8 Files

```
'Open dialog and check if successful
If dlgSave.ShowDialog = Windows.Forms.DialogResult.OK Then

    'Allocate filename
    fname = dlgSave.FileName

    'Prepare to transmit data stream
    Dim outstream As StreamWriter = New StreamWriter(fname)

    'Read text box and send data to file
    outstream.WriteLine(TextBox1.Text)

    'Close file
    outstream.Close()

    End If
End Sub
```

Let us now take it line by line so that we can understand what is happening.

Analysing the Code

1.
```
'Declare filename variable
Dim fname As String
```

The File where the data is to be saved will have a name and a path associated with it so we need a variable available to accommodate that information.

2.
```
'Declare save file dialog
Dim dlgSave As SaveFileDialog = New SaveFileDialog
```

SaveFileDialog is a Dialog control that will enable a file to be saved. dlgSave is a variable which is instanced, i.e. created as an object for saving a file.

3.
```
'Select save file dialog filter
dlgSave.Filter = "Text Files|*.txt|All Files|*.*"
```

Files 8

This restricts the type of files that are displayed. Normally only Text files are displayed but *All Files* can be displayed if required.

4.
```
'Open dialog and check if successful
If dlgSave.ShowDialog = Windows.Forms.DialogResult.OK Then
```

Once a file has been selected or created, a check is made to see that it is available for data to be written to it. If successful it then proceeds to the next line.

5.
```
'Allocate filename
fname = dlgSave.FileName
```

The filename and path are now extracted and stored in the variable *fname*.

6,
```
'Prepare to transmit data stream
Dim outstream As IO.StreamWriter = New IO.StreamWriter(fname)
```

This is the line where System.IO is important. *IO.StreamWriter* is responsible for the process of initiating writing to the file. Outstream is a variable which is an object and is instanced with the location of the file which is to be written to.

7.
```
'Read text box and send data to file
outstream.WriteLine(TextBox1.Text)
```

This is the crux of the code. Here the text data is written to the file. Using *WriteLine* ensures all the information in that line is transmitted.

8.
```
'Close file
outstream.Close()
```

It is essential that the file is closed otherwise it can become corrupted and it would be impossible ever to access the data in the future.

As you type in the code, drop-down menus will continually appear and there will be circumstances in the future when you will have the

8   Files

opportunity to try out some of the alternatives. For the moment we need to test the program

Running Example 8.1

When the program is running, type a short statement into the text box (Figure 8.2).

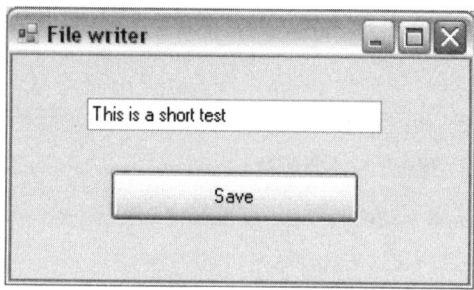

Figure 8.2 The Form running

Now click on the Save button and obtain the SaveAs window (Figure 8.3). This is identical to the one that you have encountered many times before in Windows Applications. It has been implemented by *SaveFileDialog* in the code.

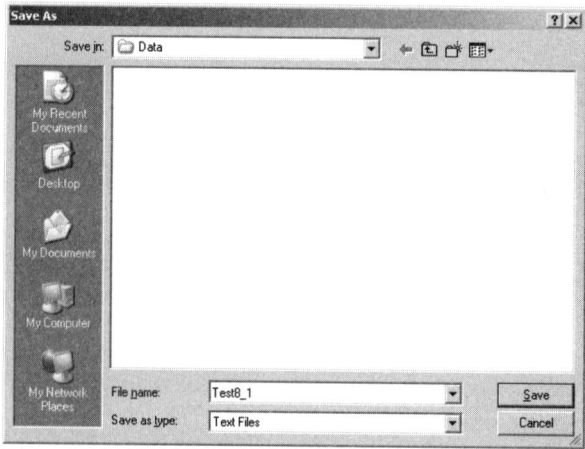

Figure 8.3 The SaveAs window

Type in a File name and make sure that it is pertinent to what is being saved. It is possible to overwrite an existing file but at least you will be given the opportunity to decide whether or not you wish to. Once you are satisfied that you have the correct name, which in our case is Test 8_1.txt, click on *Save*. You can now close Example 8.1.

The next stage is to recover the data.

Checking the Data on File

Before we write the recover data program we can check the contents of Test 8.1.txt using Notepad or a similar text editor. Open Test 8_1.txt in Notepad and you should obtain the statement; *This is a short test* (Figure 8.4).

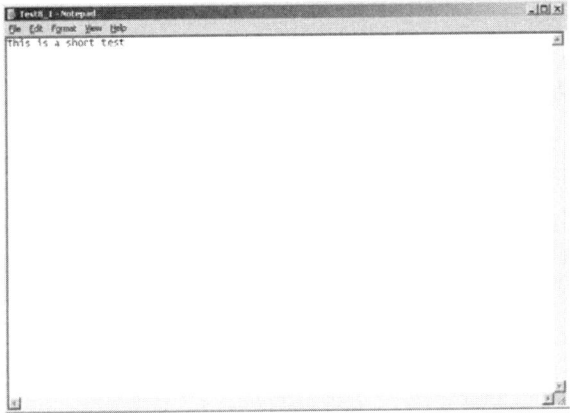

Figure 8.4 Checking the contents of Test8_1.txt

Example 8.2

To some extent the recovery or reading of the data is the converse of the writing process. The mechanics are basically the same with *Save* being replaced by *Open*, *Write* by *Read* and *out* by *in*. Example 8.2 illustrates what is meant.

Start up a Visual Basic 2005 Express New Project and call it Example 8.2. Figure 8.5 shows the layout of the Form which again consists of a text box and a button. The Text for the Form is changed to *File reader* and that for the button to *Open*.

8 Files

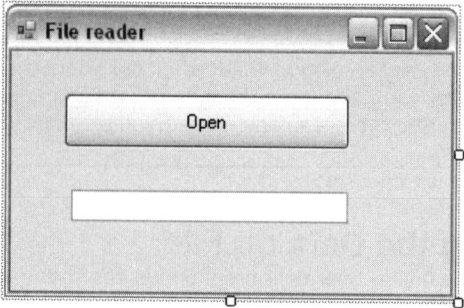

Figure 8.5 Example 8.2 Form

The Code

This code is again inserted in Button1_Click and should now have some familiarity in its structure.

```
Private Sub Button1_Click(ByVal sender As System.Object, ByVal e As System.EventArgs) Handles Button1.Click

    'Declare filename variable
    Dim fname As String
    'Declare open file dialog
    Dim dlgOpen As OpenFileDialog = New OpenFileDialog
    'Select open file dialog filter
    dlgOpen.Filter = "Text Files|*.txt|All Files|*.*"

    'Open dialog and check if successful
    If dlgOpen.ShowDialog = Windows.Forms.DialogResult.OK Then
        'Allocate filename
        fname = dlgOpen.FileName
        'Prepare to receive data stream
        Dim instream As StreamReader = New StreamReader(fname)
        'Data stream read from file and displayed
        TextBox1.Text = instream.ReadLine
        'Close file
        instream.Close()
    End If

End Sub
```

Files 8

The main process is to locate a file and set it up for the data to be written directly into the text box.

The statement *TextBox1.Text = instream.ReadLine* reads the line of text.

System.IO

Do not forget to add *Imports system.io* at the top of the code.

> Imports system.io
>
> Public Class Form1

Running Example 8.2

When the program is run, the Open button should be clicked to bring up the Open window (Figure 8.6).

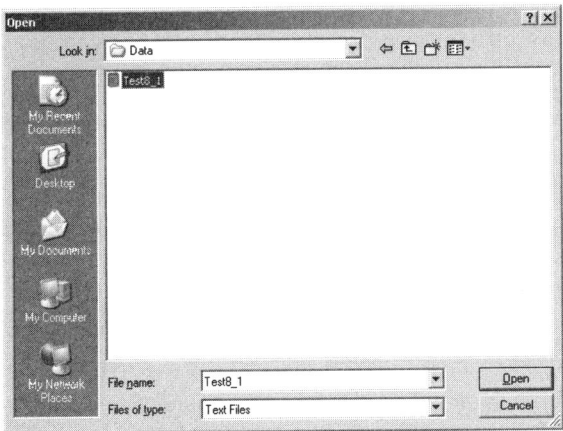

Figure 8.6 The Open window

When Test8_1.txt is selected, the statement *This is a short test* will appear in the text box (Figure 8.7).

8 Files

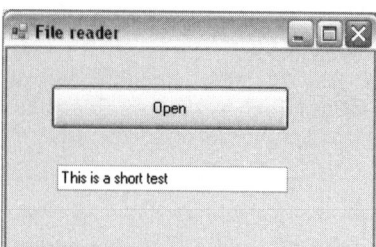

Figure 8.7 Testing Example 8.2

Exercise 8.1

Test Examples 8.1 and 8.2 in their ability to save and recover text data, i.e. using different statements.

Handling Numerical Data

Numerical data is dealt with in a similar manner to text as far as saving to a file is concerned. The only problem lies in acquiring the data in the first place. If data is being captured at a fairly slow rate it is possible to open, save and close the file as required but in so doing each time the data is stored it will overwrite the data that is already in the file. This happens with sequential files with which we are dealing. This problem does not occur with random access files but as has already been stated this is beyond the scope of this book.

We therefore have to acquire data, temporarily store it and then save it. Fortunately there is a mathematical function which will assist us to perform this task and it is called an *Array*.

Arrays

We encountered arrays in the previous chapter when we stored some numbers prior to displaying them. An array is a series of numbers which can be allocated into compartments. Each compartment is called an element which can be identified with a number. Figure 8.8 shows a 10-element array with each element identified.

Element	0	1	2	3	4	5	6	7	8	9
Contents	25	56	43	6	78	34	57	21	34	89

Figure 8.8 A 10-element array

There are some important points to note. Firstly, element 0 is the first number and element 9 is the tenth number. Secondly, the contents are identified by the element number. This means that elements 3, 6 and 7 are respectively 6, 57 and 21.

Figure 8.8 shows a one-dimensional (1D) array. Arrays can be multidimensional. A two-dimensional array consists of rows and columns (Figure 8.9) and is the normal format of a spreadsheet.

	Column 1	*Column 2*	*Column 3*
Row 1	24	67	35
Row 2	54	22	89
Row 3	23	12	45

Figure 8.9 A two-dimensional array

When used with Visual Basic 2005 Express it is important to declare the array and this is done with the following statement:

Dim A(10) as Integer

This is a 10-element array of integers. A two-dimensional array is declared as A(3,10) which is 3 columns and 10 rows. Remember the first element in either direction will be 0.

Example 8.3

This program generates 10 random numbers, stores them in an array and then displays them in a text box. When they are stored the number of elements being stored is saved along with the date and time. The 10 numbers are then saved in elements 0 to 9 of the array. The number of elements and the data and time are often referred to as a header file and are useful for saving information that is needed alongside the original data. Sometimes header files contain information about the units of the data, temperature at which the data is collected or any other information which may be of use. The format of the header file must be known before data can be extracted from the file.

Create a new project and call it Example 8.3. Figure 8.10 shows the layout of the Form. It contains a text box and three buttons with their Text Properties changed to *Generate*, *Save* and *Exit*. The Multiline

8 Files

Property is changed to True so that the text box can be enlarged. The Text Property of the Form is changed to *Random number writer*.

Figure 8.10 Example 8.3 Form

The Code

We shall initially consider the code for the buttons before adding the Declarations and the Form_Load.

The Buttons

Buttons enable the 10 random numbers to be generated and displayed, the numbers to be saved and the program to be ended. Note that j is associated with the element numbers, i.e. 0 to 9.

Generate

```
Private Sub Button1_Click(ByVal sender As System.Object, ByVal e
As System.EventArgs) Handles Button1.Click

   'Make B a null string
   B = ""
   'Loop
   For j = 0 To (num – 1)
      'Generate random number
      A(j) = Int(Rnd() * 100)
      'Add to string with CR & LF
      B = B + Str(A(j)) & Chr(13) & Chr(10)
   Next
```

```
'Display string
TextBox1.Text() = B

End Sub
```

This code creates 10 random numbers which are multiplied by 100 and Int() is used before being stored in elements 0 to 9 of an array. These numbers are also concatenated into a string B. Each term has a carriage return (Chr(13)) and a line feed (Chr(10)) added to it such that each number occupies its own line when it is displayed.

Chr() converts a number into its equivalent ASCII code. It has already been explained that ASCII can be used to represent the keys of a keyboard and that includes all of the control characters that are used in printers as well. One key, the enter key, performs two tasks. Firstly it returns the screen cursor back to the beginning of a line and secondly it moves the cursor down to the next line. These two actions are called a carriage return (CR) plus a line feed (LF). *13* is the ASCII for carriage return; *10* is the line feed. CR+LF is a very common attachment to data which is produced by instruments and it is something that computer programs that deal with data must be able to handle.

Save

This code is similar to the save routine that we encountered in Example 8.1. Inside a single *outstream.Writeline* statement of that program we have two statements which output the number of random numbers being saved and the current date and time. The random numbers are saved one at a time using the *outstream.Writeline* statement.

```
Private Sub Button2_Click(ByVal sender As System.Object, ByVal e As System.EventArgs) Handles Button2.Click

    'Declare filename variable
    Dim fname As String

    'Declare save file dialog
    Dim dlgSave As SaveFileDialog = New SaveFileDialog

    'Select save file dialog filter
    dlgSave.Filter = "Text Files|*.txt|All Files|*.*"

    'Open dialog and check if successful
    If dlgSave.ShowDialog = Windows.Forms.DialogResult.OK Then
```

8 Files

```vbnet
    'Allocate filename
    fname = dlgSave.FileName


    'Prepare to transmit data stream
    Dim outstream As StreamWriter = New StreamWriter(fname)

    'Transmit count number
    outstream.WriteLine(num)

    'Dimemension Date Time
    Dim myDate As DateTime = Now

    'Transmit Date & Time
    outstream.WriteLine(myDate)

    'Data loop
    For j = 0 To (num – 1)
       'Send data to file
       outstream.WriteLine(A(j))
    Next

    'Close file
    outstream.Close()

  End If

End Sub
```

Exit

This is our normal end of program code.

```vbnet
Private Sub Button3_Click(ByVal sender As System.Object, ByVal e As System.EventArgs) Handles Button3.Click

  'End program
  End

End Sub
```

Form_Load

This code allocates the number of random numbers that are to be stored and re-seeds the random number generator.

```
Private Sub Form1_Load(ByVal sender As System.Object, ByVal e
As System.EventArgs) Handles MyBase.Load

   'Number of random numbers to capture
   num = 10
   'Randomize the random number generator
   Randomize()

End Sub
```

Declarations

There are a number variables which need to be declared including the array A.

```
Imports system.io

Public Class Form1

   Dim j As Integer
   Dim num As Integer
   Dim A(10) As Integer
   Dim B As String
```

Running Example 8.3

When the program is run it is a case of clicking the Generate button to produce the random numbers (Figure 8.11).

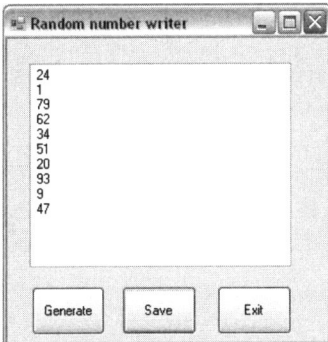

Figure 8.11 Random numbers generated

8 Files

These 10 random numbers are saved in Test8.3.txt when the Save button is clicked. The program can then be terminated with the End button.

Notepad can then be used to check the format of the stored data (Figure 8.12).

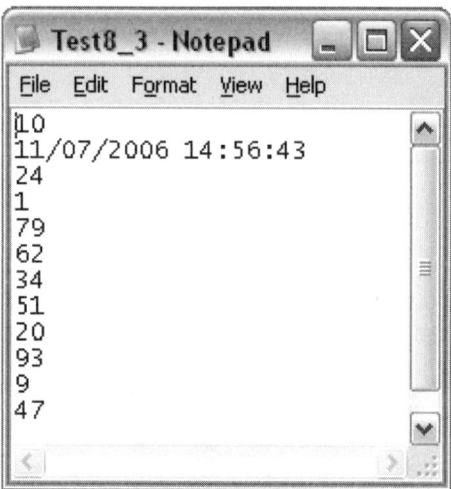

Figure 8.12 The data stored in Test8.3.txt

The number of For...Next loops is in the first line of the data and the date and time are in the second line. The random numbers then each occupy their own lines as would be expected from using the outstream.Writeline statement. The program that we now write to recover this data must adhere to this format.

Example 8.4

Create a new project and call it Example 8.4. The layout of the Form is shown in Figure 8.13. It consists of a button, 2 labels and 3 text boxes.

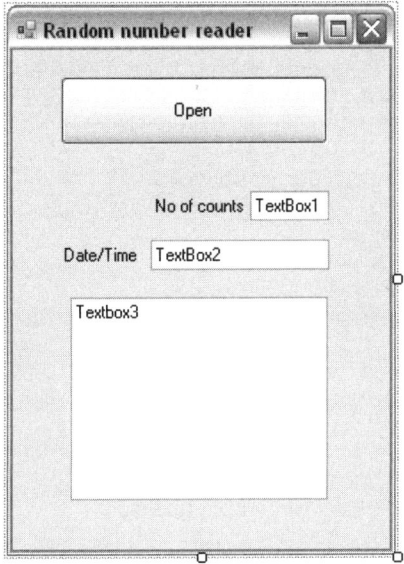

Figure 8.13 Layout of the Example 8.4 Form

The Text property of the Form is changed to *Random number reader* and that of the button is changed to *Open*. The Text properties of the labels are *No of counts* and *Date / Time* as shown in Figure 8.13. The Multiline property of TextBox3 is made *True.*

The Code

The only code is activated by the Open Button. It is basically identical to the code of Example 8.2 with the exception of reading two lines of data prior to reading 10 random numbers.

```
Private Sub Button1_Click(ByVal sender As System.Object, ByVal e As System.EventArgs) Handles Button1.Click

    'Declare variables
    Dim fname As String
    Dim j As Integer
    Dim B As String
    Dim num As Integer
```

8 Files

```
'Declare open file dialog
Dim dlgOpen As OpenFileDialog = New OpenFileDialog
'Select open file dialog filter
dlgOpen.Filter = "Text Files|*.txt|All Files|*.*"

'Open dialog and check if successful
If dlgOpen.ShowDialog = Windows.Forms.DialogResult.OK Then
   'Allocate filename
   fname = dlgOpen.FileName
   'Prepare to receive data stream
   Dim instream As StreamReader = New StreamReader(fname)

   'Read number count
   TextBox1.Text = instream.ReadLine
   num = TextBox1.Text

   'Read date and time
   TextBox2.Text = instream.ReadLine

   'Make B a null string
   B = ""
   'Loop
   For j = 0 To (num – 1)
      'Data stream read from file and displayed
      B = B + instream.ReadLine & Chr(13) & Chr(10)
   Next
   'Display data
   TextBox3.Text = B

   'Close file
   instream.Close()

End If

End Sub
```

Reading the No of counts and the Date/Time is not dissimilar to reading the text in Example 8.2. Reading and displaying 10 random numbers is more complicated.

We use a *For… Next* loop to cycle through the random numbers and we concatenate them into a string. As we wish to display them as a list we again use the two functions Chr(13) and Chr(10).

After receiving all of the data, the file is closed.

System.IO

Once again add *Imports system.io* at the top of the code.

```
Imports system.io
Public Class Form1
```

Running Example 8.4

When we run the program and click on Open we will be asked for the name of file that we wish to load. When we load Test8_3.txt we obtain the set of results shown in Figure 8.14.

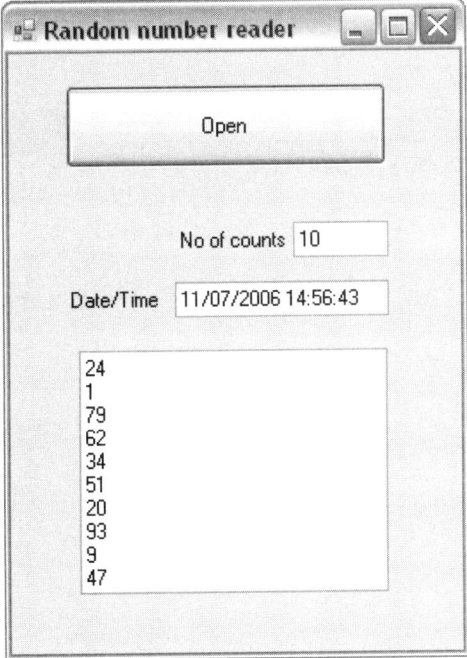

Figure 8.14 Example 8.4 results

8 Files

Storing Data in an Alternative Format

Data can be stored in many ways and also can be of indeterminate length. Header files as we used in Example 8.3 solve many of these problems by providing information which can be used to write the programs to extract the data. A very common example of this is the bit-map files of images which contain 57 pieces of information in the header file before all the data which is used to construct the image itself. Image files require a book in their own right so we shall generate some data which we cannot predict the length of and see how we can capture and display it.

We shall complicate the problem slightly by separating our data by commas rather than carriage returns and line feeds. This will create a Comma Separated File (CSF) which is commonly used for data in spreadsheets. It is not the easiest type of data for a programmer to handle except with some powerful tools available for string handling.

Example 8.5

This program will produce an unknown number of data points which will be saved to file. Create a new project and call it Example 8.5. Lay out the Form as shown in Figure 8.15.

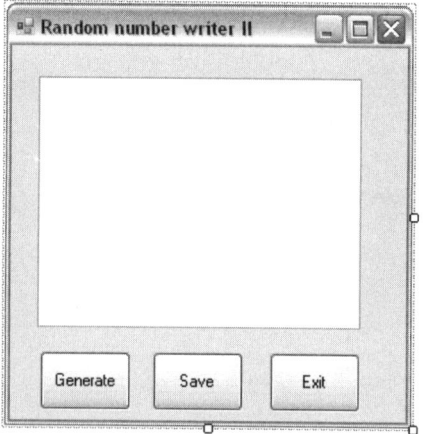

Figure 8.15 Layout of Example 8.5 Form

This Form has an identical layout of text box and three buttons to the Form for Example 8.3. The only difference is the Form Text which is *Random number writer II*. If you wish you can copy Example 8.3 and change the relevant files to Example 8.5.

Once you have laid out the form you can then look at the code.

The Code

There are many similarities in the Code of Example 8.5 with that of Example 8.3. The main differences are that we do not have a header file nor generate a fixed number of random numbers. Also we do require a Form_Load sub routine. Let us look at the Generate button code.

Generate

```
Private Sub Button1_Click(ByVal sender As System.Object, ByVal e As System.EventArgs) Handles Button1.Click

    'Make B a null string
    B = ""
    're-seed random number generator
    Randomize()
    'Loop
    Do Until A = 59
        'Generate random number
        A = Int(Rnd() * 100)
        'Add to string with comma
        B = B + Str(A) + ","
    Loop
    'Display string
    TextBox1.Text() = B

End Sub
```

The loop that we use in the example is a *Do Until...Loop*. This type of loop continues until a particular situation is found to be true. In this case we arbitrarily select the number 59 (it can be any number between 0 and 100) and then cycle the loop until that random number is generated. It may only be a few cycles or it could be hundreds. This produces the unpredictable number of data points that we require for this example.

8 Files

We also concatenate the random numbers into a string with each data point separated by a comma. When the string is displayed it should wrap around several lines.

The remaining code is similar to Example 8.3 with one exception.

Save

This exception is in the Save sub-routine. All our data, no matter how long it is, is contained in the string variable B. Technically one line, it can be written to the file in the single statement; *outstream.WriteLine(B)*. This shows how straightforward it is to store data as all of the other code is now very familiar to us and has not been changed from either of the two examples, Example 8.1 and Example 8.3.

```
Private Sub Button2_Click(ByVal sender As System.Object, ByVal e As System.EventArgs) Handles Button2.Click

    'Declare filename variable
    Dim fname As String

    'Declare save file dialog
    Dim dlgSave As SaveFileDialog = New SaveFileDialog

    'Select save file dialog filter
    dlgSave.Filter = "Text Files|*.txt|All Files|*.*"

    'Open dialog and check if successful
    If dlgSave.ShowDialog = Windows.Forms.DialogResult.OK Then

        'Allocate filename
        fname = dlgSave.FileName

        'Prepare to transmit data stream
        Dim outstream As StreamWriter = New StreamWriter(fname)

        'Send data to file
        outstream.WriteLine(B)

        'Close file
        outstream.Close()

    End If

End Sub
```

End

This is the usual code for the Exit button.

```
Private Sub Button3_Click(ByVal sender As System.Object, ByVal e As System.EventArgs) Handles Button3.Click

    'End program
    End

End Sub
```

Declarations

Note that A is a simple variable *not* an array as in Example 8.3. *Imports system.io* has again been added.

```
Imports system.io

Public Class Form1

Dim j As Integer
Dim A As Integer
Dim B As String
```

Running Example 8.5

When we run this program we obtain a set of data which may cover one or several lines (Figure 8.16). This data is saved in Test8_5.txt.

Figure 8.16 The multilines of data

8 Files

When we close this program we can then consider how we can recover and display this data.

Example 8.6

The data that this example has to handle is typical of the data that spreadsheets such as Microsoft Excel handle as a matter of course. If you were to load Test8.5.txt into an Excel spreadsheet you would use a wizard to enable all of the data separated by commas to be placed into individual cells. That is the task that we wish Example 8.6 to perform. We will not use cells but we will have the data displayed on separate lines.

Create a new project and call it Example 8.6. The Form layout consists of a button and a multiline text box with scrollbars (Figure 8.17). The *Form Text* is *File reader II*.

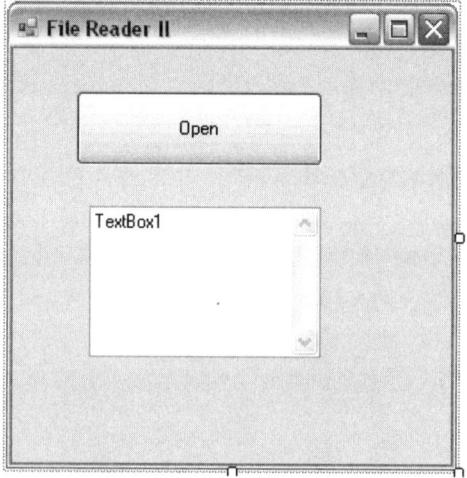

Figure 8.17 Layout of File reader II

The code for Example 8.6 is again similar to that of the previous examples for reading files.

The Code

The only code for this example is restricted to the sub-routine associated with the Open button. The principal difference in this code to what we have used before is the process of reading the data.

Previously we have read the data in line by line. This time we do not know how much data is present and so we read the data in as a complete unit by reading up to the end of the file by using *instream.ReadToEnd*. The data is then placed in a string variable B which can either be displayed as a string or alternatively split at each comma.

The process of splitting is shown by using the String.Replace() function. In this case the comma is replaced by *Carriage Return + Line Return* which will give us the data presented in a line by line sequence.

```
Private Sub Button1_Click(ByVal sender As System.Object, ByVal e As System.EventArgs) Handles Button1.Click

    'Declare variables
    Dim fname As String
    Dim j As Integer
    Dim B As String

    'Declare open file dialog
    Dim dlgOpen As OpenFileDialog = New OpenFileDialog

    'Select open file dialog filter
    dlgOpen.Filter = "Text Files|*.txt|All Files|*.*"

    'Open dialog and check if successful
    If dlgOpen.ShowDialog = Windows.Forms.DialogResult.OK Then

        'Allocate filename
        fname = dlgOpen.FileName

        'Prepare to receive data stream
        Dim instream As StreamReader = New StreamReader(fname)

        'Data stream read to end of file
        B = instream.ReadToEnd
```

8 Files

```
    'Dimension variable as string and load data
    Dim Bstring As String = B

    'Display data after replacing commas with CR & LF
    TextBox1.Text = Bstring.Replace(",", Chr(13) & Chr(10))

    'Close file
    instream.Close()

  End If

End Sub
```

After the following Exercise we can test the code.

Exercise 8.2

Have you got any errors in the Error List?
Have you remembered to add *Imports system.io* to the beginning of the code.

Running Example 8.6

When we load Test8_5.txt into Example 8.6 we shall get the data displayed as in Figure 8.18. As the data occupies more lines than displayed in the text box it is important to use the scroll bars to view all of the data.

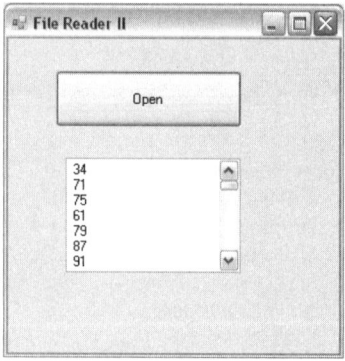

Figure 8.18 Displaying the Test8_5.txt

Exercise 8.3

Use Example 8.6 to view the data stored in the other data files that have been produced in this chapter.

Summary

This chapter has shown how data can be saved to and retrieved from files. It has been shown that once the basic code has been written it only requires slight modifications to accommodate a range of different formats of data. You will find that it is fairly easy to adapt this code to a wide range of applications that you will encounter in the future. The important rule is to document each part and try to keep the file handling code separate from the data processing section. You will find that the code is very much easier to maintain under these circumstances.

8 Files

9
Bars and Pies

In Chapter 7 we learnt how to plot graphs using Picture boxes. Line graphs are just one of the pictorial representations that we use for data and in this chapter we shall look at some others. In many applications that handle data, e.g. Microsoft Excel, bar charts and pie charts are often used. In many respects these methods of representing data are easier to understand but from the programmers point of view they are more difficult to code. This chapter will show you the basics of how it may be done and provides you with some quite presentable charts in the process.

It is very important to appreciate that the type of data represented by bar and pie charts is different from that used to plot graphs. Our two example programs in this chapter demonstrate that very well.

The first example will deal with the frequency that numbers on a dice appear. These will be plotted in the form of histogram or bar chart in which the vertical axis will be rescaled as the number of throws increase. The second one will use a pie chart to represent the proportions of red, green and blue used to mix into colours. This example will also take into account that the same proportions of the primary colours do not always give the same colour on mixing.

In both cases we shall devise the code to produce the data and then we shall consider how the charts are going to be used to represent that data.

Example 9.1

Our source of data for this example will be an experiment that will simulate the throwing of a dice. We shall maintain a running total of the number of times each of the six faces on the dice is uppermost and plot a bar chart of the results as time progresses. This will use several of the techniques we have used in previous chapters and apply them to a quite different situation.

Create a new Visual Basic 2005 Express project and set out the Form as shown in Figure 9.1.

9   Bars and Pies

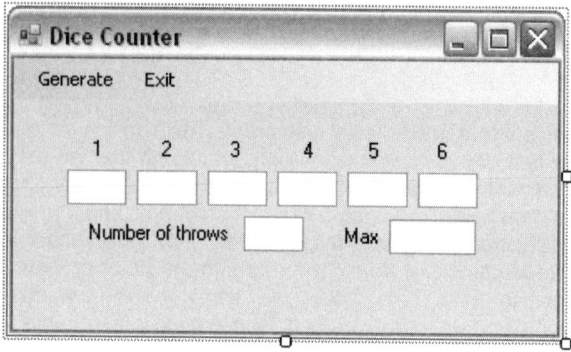

Figure 9.1 Example 9.1 Form

There are 8 Text boxes and 8 Labels. The Text for the Labels is *1, 2, 3, 4, 5, 6, Number of throws* and *Max* There is a MenuStrip with two ToolStripMenutems 1 and 2 which have their Text changed to *Generate* and *Exit* respectively. A Timer with an Interval *100* is also added. The Text of the Form is changed to *Dice counter*.

The Code

This code will be developed in stages so that in some instances the comments will be altered as the original code is integrated into the final product. We shall adopt the same principle as in previous chapters by highlighting additional code as it is introduced.

Declarations

We shall use a one-dimensional 6-element array to store the number of counts for each face of the dice. n is the total number of throws and we shall also use a variable for the calculated value of the dice. Amax is used to represent the maximum number of times that any value has occurred. This will be used later to rescale the bar chart vertical axis.

```
Public Class Form1

  'Declare variables
  Dim A(5) As Integer
  Dim n As Integer
  Dim Dice_value As Integer
  Dim Amax As Integer
```

Form_Load

We initially need to zero the 6 counter values and then display those values on the Form. The random number generator is also re-seeded.

```
Private Sub Form1_Load(ByVal sender As Object, ByVal e
As System.EventArgs) Handles Me.Load

    'Zero counters
    A(0) = 0
    A(1) = 0
    A(2) = 0
    A(3) = 0
    A(4) = 0
    A(5) = 0

    'Display counters
    TextBox1.Text = A(0)
    TextBox2.Text = A(1)
    TextBox3.Text = A(2)
    TextBox4.Text = A(3)
    TextBox5.Text = A(4)
    TextBox6.Text = A(5)

    'Declare initialvalues
    Amax = 0

    'Reseed random number generate
    Randomize()

End Sub
```

MenuStrip

These are both short sub-routines, Generate ToolStripMenuItem initiates the timer and Exit ToolStripMenuItem closes the program after switching off the timer.

Generate ToolStripMenuItem

```
Private Sub GenerateToolStripMenuItem_Click(ByVal sender
As System.Object, ByVal e As System.EventArgs)
Handles GenerateToolStripMenuItem.Click

    'Start timer
    Timer1.Enabled = True
```

9 Bars and Pies

```
End Sub
```

Exit ToolStripMenuItem

```
Private Sub ExitToolStripMenuItem_Click(ByVal sender As
Object, ByVal e As System.EventArgs) Handles
ExitToolStripMenuItem.Click

    'Switch off timer
    Timer1.Enabled = False

    'End program
    End

End Sub
```

Timer

This sub-routine is called every 100ms and results in a throw of the dice. The equation used to simulate the dice is :

Dice_value = Int(Rnd(1) * 6) + 1

The integer of the random number, Rnd(), multiplied by 6 produces numbers between 0 and 5 and addition of 1 gives us the range 1 to 6 as required.

The storage of the number of throws for each dice number coupled with the update on the Form is effected by a Select Case structure. The bar will be plotted by calling the *Plotgraph* sub-routine.

```
Private Sub Timer1_Tick(ByVal sender As Object, ByVal e As
System.EventArgs) Handles Timer1.Tick

    'Value of dice
    Dice_value = Int(Rnd(1) * 6) + 1

    'Number of throws
    n = n + 1

    'Display number of throws
    TextBox7.Text = n
```

```
    ' Select Case Dice_value
    Case 1
       A(0) = A(0) + 1
       TextBox1.Text = A(0)
    Case 2
       A(1) = A(1) + 1
       TextBox2.Text = A(1)
    Case 3
       A(2) = A(2) + 1
       TextBox3.Text = A(2)
    Case 4
       A(3) = A(3) + 1
       TextBox4.Text = A(3)
    Case 5
       A(4) = A(4) + 1
       TextBox5.Text = A(4)
    Case 6
       A(5) = A(5) + 1
       TextBox6.Text = A(5)
       'Plot graph
       Plotgraph()

  End Select

End Sub
```

Plotgraph

This is sub-routine which we can easily create ourselves. Type in *Private Sub Plotgraph* at the end of the program between the last *End Sub* and *End Class* and the sub-routine is automatically generated.

```
End Sub

Private Sub Plotgraph()

End Sub

End Class
```

This sub-routine will contain the details to plot the bar chart but for the time being we shall use it to generate the maximum number of times a dice value has occurred.

9 Bars and Pies

```
Private Sub Plotgraph()

   'Declare variable
   Dim j As Integer

   For j = 0 To 5
     'Determine maximum values
     If A(j) > Amax Then
        Amax = A(j)

        ' Display maximum values
        TextBox8.Text = Amax
     End If
   Next

End Sub
```

Testing the Code

Before we introduce the bar chart into the program let us make sure this code does what we require it to do. Run the program and click *Generate*. You should get each of the dice text boxes increasing in value at approximately the same rate (Figure 9.2). This should show whether the algorithm that we are using is correct.

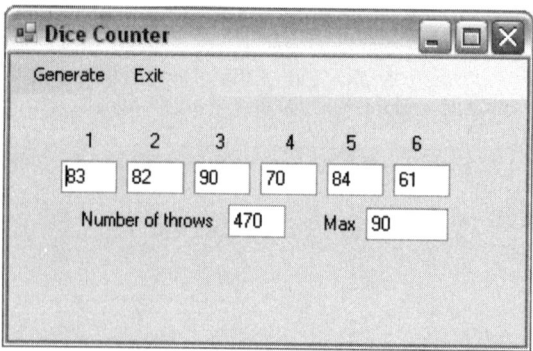

Figure 9.2 Checking the dice throwing algorithm

Adding the Bar Chart

The bar chart is now going to be added. Initially we shall place the grid on to the Form. Then we apply the data followed by the labelling of the axes. Finally we will get the vertical axis to rescale itself automatically.

Adding the PictureBox

Enlarge the Form and add a PictureBox as shown in Figure 9.3.

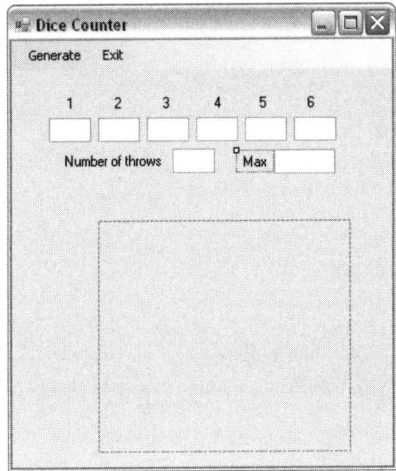

Figure 9.3 Placing the PictureBox on the Form

The grid

The grid will be drawn inside the PictureBox. All of the code will be added to the Plotgraph sub-routine. Let us add the code and then explain what it does. The unshaded rows are sections of code that we have already typed in.

```
Private Sub Plotgraph()

    'Declare graph variables
    Dim g As Graphics = PictureBox1.CreateGraphics
    Dim pen1 As New Pen(Color.Black)

    'Declare variables
    Dim j As Integer
```

9 Bars and Pies

```
'Draw graph frame
g.DrawLine(pen1, 0, 0, 180, 0)
g.DrawLine(pen1, 180, 0, 180, 160)
g.DrawLine(pen1, 180, 150, 0, 150)
g.DrawLine(pen1, 0, 160, 0, 0)

'Horizontal tick markers
For n = 1 To 5
   j = n * 30
   g.DrawLine(pen1, j, 0, j, 160)
Next

'Vertical tick markers
For n = 1 To 4
   j = n * 30
   g.DrawLine(pen1, 0, j, 180, j)
Next

'Plot dice bar chart
For j = 0 To 5

  'Determine maximum values
  If A(j) > Amax Then
     Amax = A(j)

     ' Display maximum values
     TextBox8.Text = Amax
  End If
Next

End Sub
```

The code to draw the grid is similar to that we used for our graph plotting in Chapter 7. The horizontal axis length is 180 pixels as there are 6 dice values and each face is allocated 30 pixels. Each of these 6 sub-divisions is called a *bin* and the value of the throws allocated to each dice value will be plotted within the bin. The vertical axis has a length of 150 pixels and we shall need to scale our y-values taking that into account.

Figure 9.4 shows the view of the Form with the grid displayed.

Bars and Pies 9

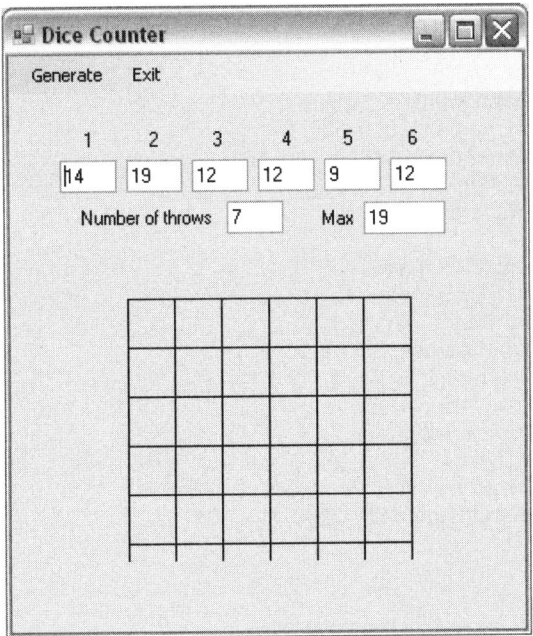

Figure 9.4 Drawing the grid

Adding throw values to the grid

This involves plotting the values in the Text boxes at the top of the Form and ensuring that they appear in the appropriate bin.

```
Private Sub Plotgraph()

'Declare graph variables
Dim g As Graphics = PictureBox1.CreateGraphics
Dim pen1 As New Pen(Color.Black)

'Declare variables
Dim j As Integer

Dim n As Integer
  Dim x1 As Integer
```

153

9   Bars and Pies

```
Dim y1 As Integer
Dim xtemp As Integer
Dim xxtemp As Integer

'Draw graph frame
  g.DrawLine(pen1, 0, 0, 180, 0)
  g.DrawLine(pen1, 180, 0, 180, 160)
  g.DrawLine(pen1, 180, 150, 0, 150)
  g.DrawLine(pen1, 0, 160, 0, 0)

'Horizontal tick markers
For n = 1 To 5
   j = n * 30
   g.DrawLine(pen1, j, 0, j, 160)
Next

'Vertical tick markers
For n = 1 To 4
   j = n * 30
   g.DrawLine(pen1, 0, j, 180, j)
Next

'Zero horizontal co-ordinate
x1 = 0

'Plot dice bar chart
For j = 0 To 5

   'Determine x-co-ordinate position
   xtemp = j * 10
   x1 = x1 + xtemp + 10

   'Determine y-height
   y1 = 150 - Int((A(j) / ymax) * 150)

   'Plot bar
   For n = 0 To 10
      g.DrawLine(pen1, x1 + n, 150, x1 + n, y1)
   Next n

   'Determine next x co-ordinate
   xxtemp = j + 1
   x1 = 20 * xxtemp
```

Bars and Pies

```
    'Determine maximum values
    If A(j) > Amax Then
       Amax = A(j)

       'Display maximum values
       TextBox8.Text = Amax
    End If
  Next

End Sub
```

Other sections of code need changing. We have to declare ymax in Declarations.

```
Public Class Form1

'Declare variables
Dim A(5) As Integer
Dim n As Integer
Dim Dice_value As Integer
Dim Amax As Integer
Dim ymax As Integer
```

Also an initial value for ymax is allocated in Form Load

```
Private Sub Form1_Load(ByVal sender As Object, ByVal e As
System.EventArgs) Handles Me.Load

   'Zero counters
   A(0) = 0
   A(1) = 0
   A(2) = 0
   A(3) = 0
   A(4) = 0
   A(5) = 0

   'Display counters
   TextBox1.Text = A(0)
   TextBox2.Text = A(1)
   TextBox3.Text = A(2)
   TextBox4.Text = A(3)
   TextBox5.Text = A(4)
   TextBox6.Text = A(5)
```

9 Bars and Pies

```
'Declare initial values
ymax = 50
Amax = 0

'Reseed random number generate
Randomize()
End Sub
```

Once these modifications have been added we will be able to display the dice throw numbers in the six bins (Figure 9.5).

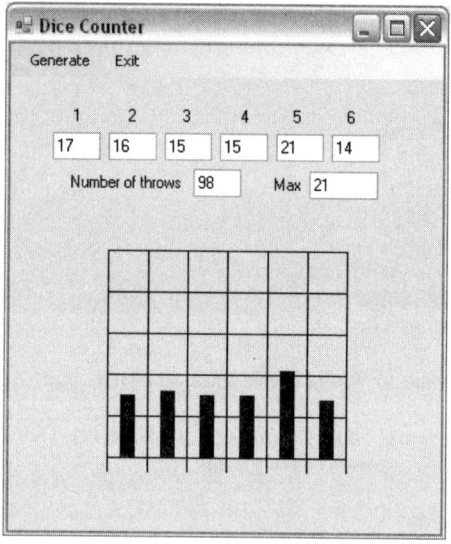

Figure 9.5 The number of dice throws displayed

We can see from Figure 9.5 that the algorithm is working correctly as we would expect each dice value to have equal probability of being obtained but the chart still needs some correctly labelled horizontal and vertical axes.

Adding Labels

The horizontal axis requires each bin to be labelled along with a suitable title. The y-axis tick marks need calibrating also with a suitable title.

Figure 9.6 shows where we need to position the labels.

Bars and Pies 9

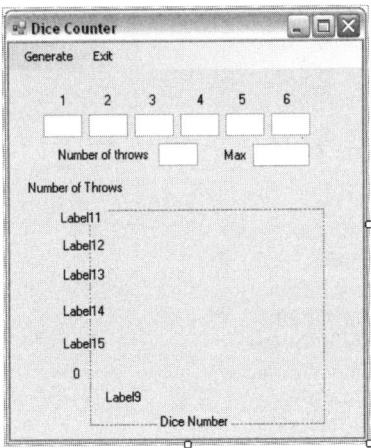

Figure 9.6 Positioning the labels on the Form

Nine labels are added to the Form. The Text for Labels 10, 16 and 17 is changed to *Dice Number*, *0* and *Number of Throws* respectively. Labels 9, 11-15 are left blank. These labels will be filled during the running of the program.

There are two sections of code that require changing. One is the Form Load section where the labels are hidden when the program starts, the other is in the Plotgraph sub-routine.

Form Load

```
Private Sub Form1_Load(ByVal sender As Object, ByVal e As
System.EventArgs) Handles Me.Load

    'Zero counters
    A(0) = 0
    A(1) = 0
    A(2) = 0
    A(3) = 0
    A(4) = 0
    A(5) = 0

    'Display counters
    TextBox1.Text = A(0)
    TextBox2.Text = A(1)
```

9 Bars and Pies

```
    TextBox3.Text = A(2)
    TextBox4.Text = A(3)
    TextBox5.Text = A(4)
    TextBox6.Text = A(5)

    'Declare initialvalues
    ymax = 50
    Amax = 0

    'Hide chart labels
    Label9.Visible = False
    Label10.Visible = False
    Label11.Visible = False
    Label12.Visible = False
    Label13.Visible = False
    Label14.Visible = False
    Label15.Visible = False
    Label16.Visible = False
    Label17.Visible = False


   'Reseed random number generate
    Randomize()

End Sub
```

Plotgraph

```
Private Sub Plotgraph()

    'Declare graph variables
    Dim g As Graphics = PictureBox1.CreateGraphics
    Dim pen1 As New Pen(Color.Black)

    'Declare variables
    Dim n As Integer
    Dim j As Integer
    Dim x1 As Integer
    Dim y1 As Integer
    Dim xtemp As Integer
    Dim xxtemp As Integer
```

```
'Dim xlabel As String
'Clear graphs
PictureBox1.Refresh()

'Initialise horizontal label
xlabel = ""

'Layout horizontal labels
For j = 1 To 6
   xlabel = xlabel + Str(j) + Space(7)
Next

'Load horizontal labels
Label9.Text = xlabel

'Load vertical labels
Label11.Text = ymax
Label12.Text = Int(ymax * 4 / 5)
Label13.Text = Int(ymax * 3 / 5)
Label14.Text = Int(ymax * 2 / 5)
Label15.Text = Int(ymax * 1 / 5)

'Display labels
Label9.Visible = True
Label10.Visible = True
Label11.Visible = True
Label12.Visible = True
Label13.Visible = True
Label14.Visible = True
Label15.Visible = True
Label16.Visible = True
Label17.Visible = True
```

```
'Draw graph frame
g.DrawLine(pen1, 0, 0, 180, 0)
g.DrawLine(pen1, 180, 0, 180, 160)
g.DrawLine(pen1, 180, 150, 0, 150)
g.DrawLine(pen1, 0, 160, 0, 0)

'Horizontal tick markers
For n = 1 To 5
   j = n * 30
   g.DrawLine(pen1, j, 0, j, 160)
```

9 Bars and Pies

```
    Next

    'Vertical tick markers
    For n = 1 To 4
       j = n * 30
       g.DrawLine(pen1, 0, j, 180, j)
    Next

    'Zero horizontal co-ordinate
    x1 = 0
    'Plot dice bar chart
    For j = 0 To 5

       'Determine x-co-ordinate position
       xtemp = j * 10
       x1 = x1 + xtemp + 10

       'Determine y-height
       y1 = 150 - Int((A(j) / ymax) * 150)

       'Plot bar
       For n = 0 To 10
          g.DrawLine(pen1, x1 + n, 150, x1 + n, y1)
       Next n

       'Determine next x co-ordinate
       xxtemp = j + 1
       x1 = 20 * xxtemp

       'Determine maximum values
       If A(j) > Amax Then
          Amax = A(j)

          'Display maximum values
          TextBox8.Text = Amax
       End If
    Next
End Sub
```

Testing the Program

Positioning the labels may require running the program several times with slightly different positions of the labels. Eventually you will succeed and obtain a Form similar to Figure 9.7 when the program is running.

Bars and Pies 9

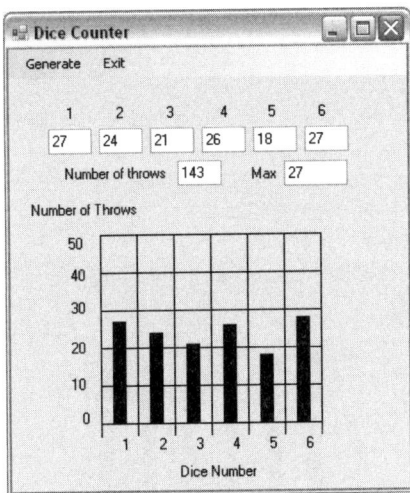

Figure 9.7 Example 9.1 running

Auto-scaling Example 9.1

The program is completed by making the vertical axis auto-scaling. This means that when any of the Number of Throws reach 50, the vertical scale is re-numbered up to 100. The process then repeats *ad-infinitum*.

The necessary code is inserted at the bottom of the Plotgraph sub-routine.

```
        'Display maximum values
        TextBox8.Text = Amax
    End If
Next


'Reset vertical axis maximum
If Amax > ymax Then
    ymax = ymax + 50
End If

End Sub
```

161

9 Bars and Pies

When the program is run, the resulting Form shown in Figure 9.8 can be obtained.

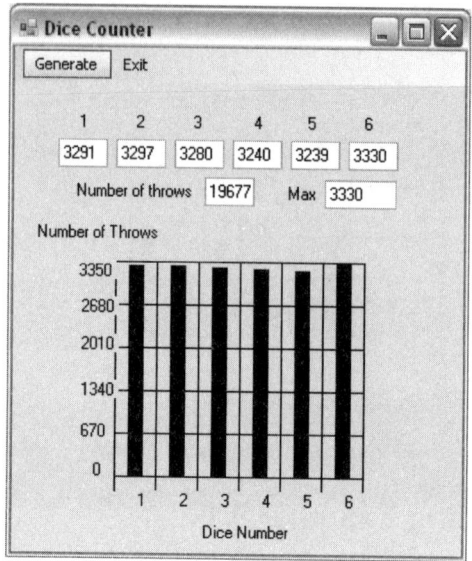

Figure 9.8 Auto-scaling in operation

Figure 9.8 illustrates how the probability of dice throwing eventually levels out.

Exercise 9.1

Select different values of *ymax* to test the auto-scaling design.

Example 9.2

Example 9.1 has illustrated how a bar chart can be created using a Picture box. Pie charts can be created in a similar way.

The problem will be tackled in a slightly different manner to that of Example 9.1. We shall again create data which can then be plotted, but the pie chart code will then be presented as a whole so that your task will be to interpret how it works. This can be done by reading the code

Bars and Pies 9

and seeing how the program works. It will be a test to see whether you can then move on to more advanced books and program code.

The data that we produce will be the proportions of red, green and blue that make up colours. Figure 9.9 shows the Form that we shall use with three horizontal Scrollbars, five Picture boxes, five Labels and three Text boxes.

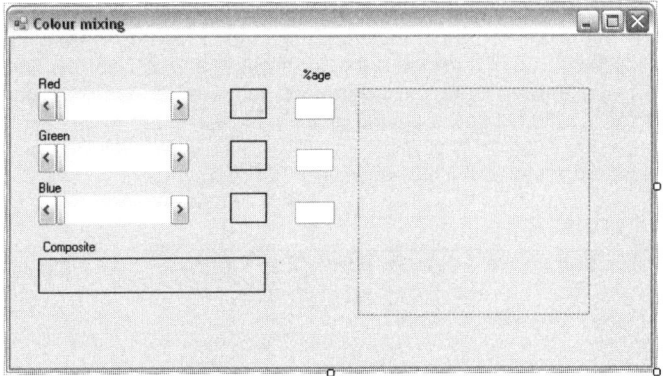

Figure 9.9 Example 9.2 Form

Picture boxes 1 – 4 have the BorderStyle property set to FixedSingle and the size of PictureBox5 is 200 x 200 pixels. The Maximum and Minimum properties of the scrollbars are 255 and 0 respectively and the Large Change is set to 1.

The Form Text is changed to *Colour mixing*, the text for the labels is as shown in Figure 9.9.

The positioning of the various components of this example is less critical than for most programs.

The sections of the code is also fairly straightforward with quite a lot of repetition.

The Code

The scrollbars are used to vary the amounts of red, green and blue colour which are going to be mixed. The colours are displayed in the adjacent picture boxes as the scroll bars are moved.

9   Bars and Pies

The syntax for loading colour into a Picture box is normally:

PictureBox1.BackColor = Color.Red

When the color is split into its composite parts the statement becomes:

PictureBox1.BackColor = Color.FromArgb(A,R,G,B)

A, R, G and B can have numbers varying between 0 and 255. In the case of A it is the degree of transparency of the colour (0 is transparent, 255 is solid). For R it denotes that 0 is black and 255 is red and the numbers in between are the degree of 'redness'. A similar argument exists for G which is green and B which is blue.

The code attached to the scrollbars is as follows:

Red Scrollbar

```
Private Sub HScrollBar1_Scroll(ByVal sender As System.Object,
ByVal e As System.Windows.Forms.ScrollEventArgs)
Handles HScrollBar1.Scroll

 'Red composition
  PictureBox1.BackColor = Color.FromArgb(255, HScrollBar1.Value,
 0, 0)

 'Red, Green, Blue mixture
  PictureBox4.BackColor = Color.FromArgb(255, HScrollBar1.Value,
  HScrollBar2.Value, HScrollBar3.Value)

 'Plot pie chart
  Pieplot()

End Sub
```

Green Scrollbar

```
Private Sub HScrollBar2_Scroll(ByVal sender As System.Object,
ByVal e As System.Windows.Forms.ScrollEventArgs)
Handles HScrollBar2.Scroll

 'Green composition
  PictureBox2.BackColor = Color.FromArgb(255, 0, HScrollBar2.Value,
0)
 'Red, Green, Blue mixture
  PictureBox4.BackColor = Color.FromArgb(255, HScrollBar1.Value,
```

```
HScrollBar2.Value, HScrollBar3.Value)

'Plot pie chart
   Pieplot()
End Sub
```

Blue Scrollbar

```
Private Sub HScrollBar3_Scroll(ByVal sender As System.Object,
ByVal e As System.Windows.Forms.ScrollEventArgs)
Handles HScrollBar3.Scroll

'Blue composition
 PictureBox3.BackColor = Color.FromArgb(255, 0, 0,
 HScrollBar3.Value)

'Red, Green, Blue mixture
 PictureBox4.BackColor = Color.FromArgb(255, HScrollBar1.Value,
 HScrollBar2.Value, HScrollBar3.Value)

'Plot pie chart
   Pieplot()
End Sub
```

The fourth Picture box is built up of all the colours set by the scrollbars. The *A* parameter is solid in all cases.

Form Load

This section of code intialises the colour in the Picture boxes.

```
Private Sub Form1_Load(ByVal sender As System.Object, ByVal e
As System.EventArgs) Handles MyBase.Load

   'Set scroll bars to maximum
   HScrollBar1.Value = 255
   HScrollBar2.Value = 255
   HScrollBar3.Value = 255

   'Fill Picture boxes with colour
   PictureBox1.BackColor = Color.FromArgb(255, HScrollBar1.Value,
   0, 0
   PictureBox2.BackColor = Color.FromArgb(255, 0,
   HScrollBar2.Value, 0)
   PictureBox3.BackColor = Color.FromArgb(255, 0, 0,
```

9 Bars and Pies

```
    HScrollBar3.Value)
    PictureBox4.BackColor = Color.FromArgb(255, HScrollBar1.Value,
    HScrollBar2.Value, HScrollBar3.Value)

End Sub
```

Testing for Colour

The code we have already written can be tested provided we add a *pieplot* sub-routine.

```
Private Sub pieplot ()

End Sub
```

No code needs to inserted into the sub-routine at the moment and we just need to check that the program works (Figure 9.10).

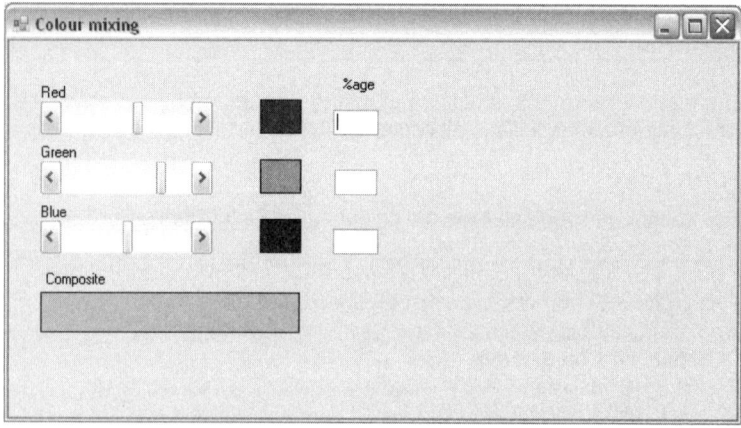

Figure 9.10 Testing the colour

The next stage of the operation is to fill in the *pieplot* sub-routine to plot the pie chart.

Bars and Pies

Drawing the pie chart

The pie chart will indicate the proportions of red, green and blue that are used to make up the colour in the Composite picture box. It is possible for the same proportions to give different colours and to accommodate this feature the diameter can change. The diameter is dependent upon the average of the percentages of the separate colours.

In order to explain how this is achieved in the program, the code for the *pieplot* sub-routine will be considered in blocks.

The first block deals with declarations.

```
Private Sub Pieplot()

    'Clear plotting area
    PictureBox5.Refresh()

    'Set up drawing parameters
    Dim g As Graphics = PictureBox5.CreateGraphics
    Dim pen1 As New Pen(Color.Red)
    Dim pen2 As New Pen(Color.Green)
    Dim pen3 As New Pen(Color.Blue)

    'Centre of pie chart co-ordinates
    Dim x1 = 100
    Dim y1 = 100

    'Declare variables
    Dim j As Integer
    Dim x2 As Integer
    Dim y2 As Integer

    Dim r0 As Integer
    Dim r1 As Integer
    Dim r2 As Integer

    Dim z As Integer

    Dim z0 As Integer
    Dim z1 As Integer
    Dim z2 As Integer

    Dim raverage As Integer
```

9 Bars and Pies

The next section reads the scroll bars and averages the values. Note the check for zero values.

```
'Obtain colour proportions
r0 = HScrollBar1.Value
r1 = HScrollBar2.Value
r2 = HScrollBar3.Value

'Average colour proportions
raverage = Int(((r0 + r1 + r2) / 3) * 100 / 255)

'Ensure radius average is non-zero
If raverage = 0 Then
   raverage = 1
End If
```

The values of the relative colour proportions are determined and turned into both percentages and angles for the pie chart.

```
'Determine colour proportions
z0 = Int(r0 * 100 / raverage)
z1 = Int(r1 * 100 / raverage)
z2 = Int(r2 * 100 / raverage)

z = z0 + z1 + z2
If z = 0 Then
   z = 1
End If

'Convert colour proportions to degrees
r0 = Int(z0 * 360 / z)
r1 = Int(z1 * 360 / z)
r2 = Int(z2 * 360 / z)
```

This following section plots the values using polar co-ordinates. The points lie on the circumference of a circle so that the pie chart will be made up of lines radiating from a central point.

```
'Plotting Red, Green, Blue pie chart

'Red proportion
For j = 0 To r0
   'x,y co-ordinates
```

```
   x2 = x1 + raverage * Math.Sin(2 * 3.142 * j / 360)
   y2 = y1 + raverage * Math.Cos(2 * 3.142 * j / 360)
   'Draw red line
   g.DrawLine(pen1, x1, y1, x2, y2)
Next

'Green proportion
For j = r0 To (r0 + r1)
   'x,y co-ordinates
   x2 = x1 + raverage * Math.Sin(2 * 3.142 * j / 360)
   y2 = y1 + raverage * Math.Cos(2 * 3.142 * j / 360)
   'Draw green line
   g.DrawLine(pen2, x1, y1, x2, y2)
Next

'Blue proportion
For j = (r0 + r1) To (r0 + r1 + r2)
   'x,y co-ordinates
   x2 = x1 + raverage * Math.Sin(2 * 3.142 * j / 360)
   y2 = y1 + raverage * Math.Cos(2 * 3.142 * j / 360)
   'Draw blue line
   g.DrawLine(pen3, x1, y1, x2, y2)
Next
```

This last section determines the relative proportions of the colour mixture in percentages and then displays them.

```
'Determine colour proportion percentages
z0 = Int(z0 * 100 / z)
z1 = Int(z1 * 100 / z)
z2 = Int(z2 * 100 / z)

'Display colour proportion percentages
TextBox1.Text = z0
TextBox2.Text = z1
TextBox3.Text = z2

End Sub
```

Exercise 9.2

Check through the code and determine how the pie chart works.

9 Bars and Pies

Running Example 9.2

This is a program that can be tested in many ways and Figures 9.11 to 9.13 show some typical results for different proportions of red, green and blue.

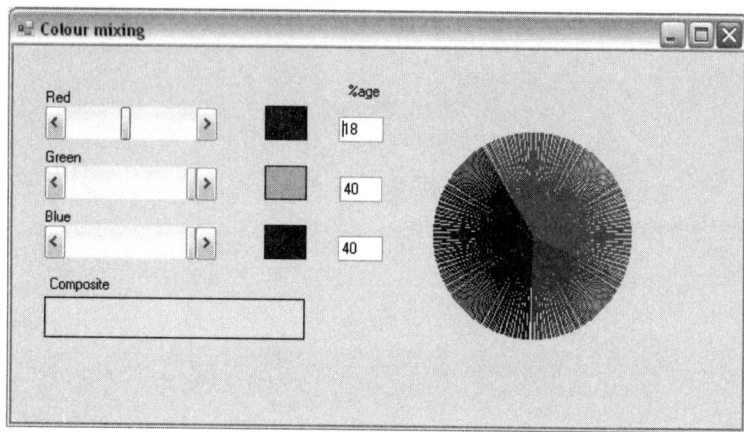

Figure 9.11 Example 9.2 running (1)

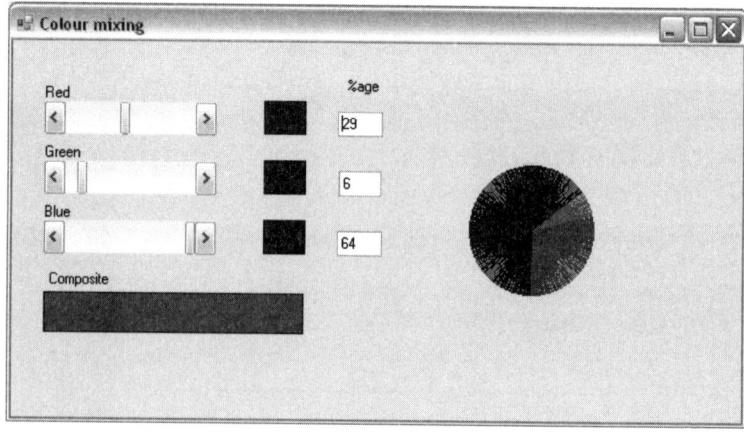

Figure 9.12 Example 9.2 running (2)

Bars and Pies 9

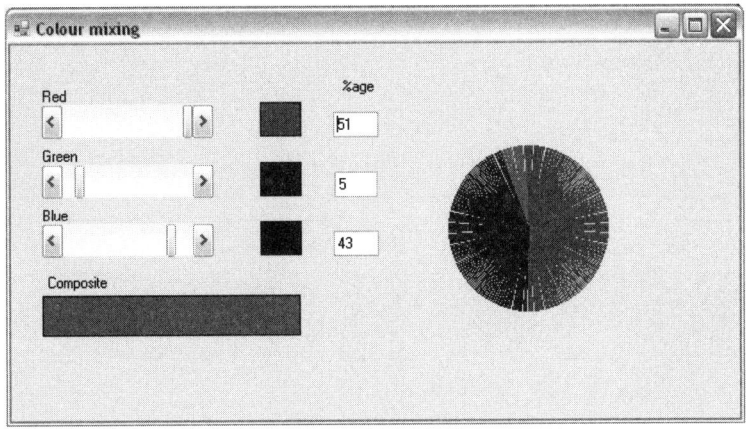

Figure 9.13 Example 9.2 running (3)

Exercise 9.3

Experiment with different proportions of red, green and blue.

Alter values of A and comment upon the effect.

Summary

This chapter has shown you how to plot bar and pie charts using a picture box. The bar chart is autoscaling and this process can be extended to line graphs as well. If you consider how the pie chart works you will realize that this is also autoscaling but in a different way.

The different methods of plotting graphs and displaying data are a valuable technique which enhances any program. You now have sufficient knowledge to write some quite complex programs but there is one other skill you need to master. How to track those elusive bugs which beset even the best-written program.

9 Bars and Pies

10
Debugging

One of the most frustrating activities in programming is trying to correct errors in programs. Certain errors such as syntax are indicated straight away but some errors including wrong results due to the incorrect construction of a program cannot be corrected since the design of the program is in the hands of the user. This chapter gives a brief overview of the debugging tools available in Visual Basic 2005 Express. More details can be obtained from either Visual Basic 2005 Express *Help* or the MSDN library.

Errors

There are three types of error:

1. Syntax errors

Some errors are the result of a statement that is incorrectly constructed, a mis-typed keyword, omitted essential punctuation or incorrect layout of a statement. These errors are indicated as each line is typed in the Error List. Double-clicking on an error in the Error List causes the cursor to jump to that position in the code so it may be corrected.

2. Run-time errors

These errors occur when a statement attempts an operation that is impossible to carry out. These can be infinite loops which will never finish or the division by zero.

3. Program design errors

These are errors which arise when the program does not perform in the way the user expects, hence producing incorrect results. Visual Basic 2005 Express will obviously have no idea what the user wants the program to do and these sorts of errors can only be corrected by an analysis of the operation of the program. This often requires a step by step approach of working through the program line by line.

The debugging tools are designed to help sort out these errors.

How to start Debugging

Everyone develops their own strategy of debugging a program. In many cases the degree of debugging required depends upon the size of

10 Debugging

program involved. One of the simplest techniques is to use textboxes to monitor variables. This method is very effective when a timer is involved and it is possible to slow a program down so that the values of variables can be checked as they appear in the textboxes. Often it is possible to detect such errors reasonably quickly and then it is necessary to seek alternative methods to solve the problems. The major disadvantage of this technique is the vast number of textboxes which can be put on to the Form and they all have to be removed once the error has been found.

The IDE Menu

Visual Basic 2005 Express provides a Debug menu in the menu bar at the top of the IDE screen (Figure 10.1).

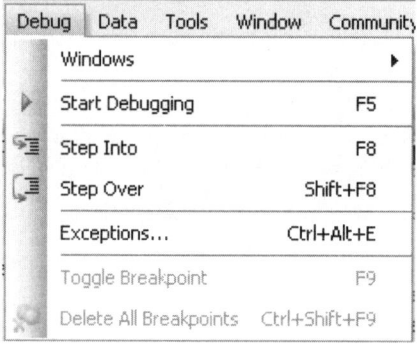

Figure 10.1 The Debug Menu

This menu contains several useful features which can help with debugging. The most important one is *Start* or its short-cut key F5 which starts the program running. A program cannot be debugged unless it is running in the Debug state. Other useful features are *Step Into, Step Over* and *New Breakpoints* which we will deal with later.

The Debug Toolbar

Visual Basic 2005 Express has a Debug Toolbar which is shown in Figure 10.2.

Debugging 10

Figure 10.2 The Debug Toolbar

This Toolbar can be displayed by selecting **View>Toolbars** from the Menu bar and then clicking on **Debug**. The functions and short cuts for the buttons on the Toolbar are shown in Table 10.1.

▶	Start Debugging	F5
‖	Break All	Ctrl+Break
■	Stop Debugging	Ctrl+Alt+Break
	Step Into	F8
	Step Over	Shift+F8
	Step Out	Ctrl+Shift+F8

Table 10.1 The Debug toolbar buttons

The *Start, Break All* and *Stop Debugging* buttons are the main buttons when running a Visual Basic 2005 Express program. The remaining buttons are used once the program has stopped and you are actively seeking the fault within the program.

Stopping the Program

Effectively there are four methods of stopping a program once it has started to run. One is a run-time error which will bring the program to a grinding halt and another is using the *Break All* button. Both these methods of halting the program are the result of some reaction within the program.

The other two methods are designed to halt the program at a pre-determined point. A simple method is to place a *Stop* statement in the program, i.e.

10 Debugging

```
        Case 6
            A(5, 1) = A(5, 1) + 1
            TextBox6.Text = A(5, 1)
    End Select

Stop

'Plot graph
    If n / 10 = Int(n / 10) Then
```

This Stop will halt the program at the end of a Case structure so that the situation can be reviewed. The disadvantage of this method is that like inserting textboxes on to the Form you may end with many Stop statements which will require deletion once the debugging process is over. It is very easy to miss a Stop statement and for it only to reappear at an inappropriate time when the program is running.

The final method of stopping a program in the Debug state is the *breakpoint*. A breakpoint is inserted by double-clicking in the grey area adjacent to the line where you wish the break to take place (Figure 10.3).

```
            TextBox5.Text = A(4)
        Case 6
            A(5) = A(5) + 1
            TextBox6.Text = A(5)
            'Plot graph
```

Figure 10.3 Inserting a breakpoint

What to do when the Program stops

Whichever method you use to pause the program, you then have to decide how you are going to deal with the situation. If you move the cursor over the lines of code which have already been executed you will find some interesting information being displayed in tip pointers (Figure 10.4).

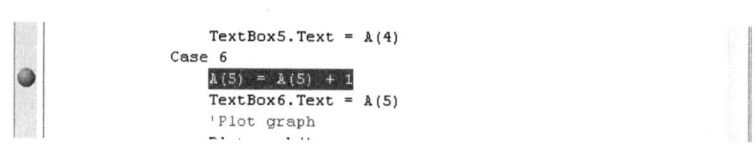

```
'Zero horizontal co-ordinate
x1 = 0

'Plot dice bar chart
For j = 0 To 5
```

Figure 10.4 Checking values of variables using the tip pointer

As the cursor passes over the variables you can determine whether or not the values being displayed are reasonable.

Keeping the Program running

Each time you press F8, the program will run to the next breakpoint and as the program pauses you can check the status of the variables.

In order to move to the next lines of code, *Step* buttons can be used. Their functions are as follows:

Step Into

This instructs the debugger to execute the next line of code. If there is a function call, *Step Into* executes the call and then stops at the first line inside the function. *Step Into* is used to look inside a function.

Step Over

This instructs the debugger to execute the next line of code. If there is a function call, *Step Over* executes the entire function and then halts at the first line outside the function call. *Step over* avoids stepping into a function.

Step Out

This is used inside a function and indicates that you wish to return to the calling function. *Step Out* will continue keeping the program running until the function returns and will break at the calling point in the calling function.

The best way of understanding the Step buttons is to use them and discover what they actually do.

Managing Breakpoints

As you develop your debugging skills you invariable start to insert breakpoints all over your code. It is in this area where Visual Basic 2005 Express lacks some of the facilities of Visual Basic 2005 Standard or Professional as it does not possess a Breakpoints window. This window in the other versions keeps track of what breakpoints have been set but in the Express version it is a case of manually checking the program as to where breakpoints have been set.

10 Debugging

By clicking on the checkboxes on the left-hand side of the window it is possible to switch off the breakpoints. To clear breakpoints permanently from the code you can use *Clear All Breakpoints* in the **Debug** menu or **Ctrl+Shift+F9**.

Debugging Windows

When you click on Debug>Windows whilst debugging you will get a sub-menu containing a number of windows (Figure 10.5).

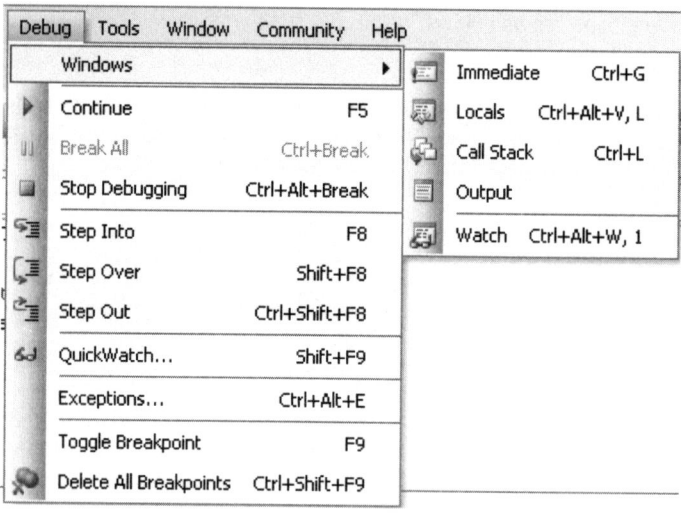

Figure 10.5 Windows available whilst debugging

Let us look at these windows in the order of their usefulness, though it must be admitted that some people may find one particular type more useful than all of the others.

The Watch Window

The Watch window monitors the variables within the program. There are various ways of instantiating, i.e. activating, this window but the most reliable way of achieving it is to run the program and then pause it. Select a suitable breakpoint point and then right-click on the highlighted variable you wish to monitor. This brings up a drop-down menu (Figure 10.6).

Debugging 10

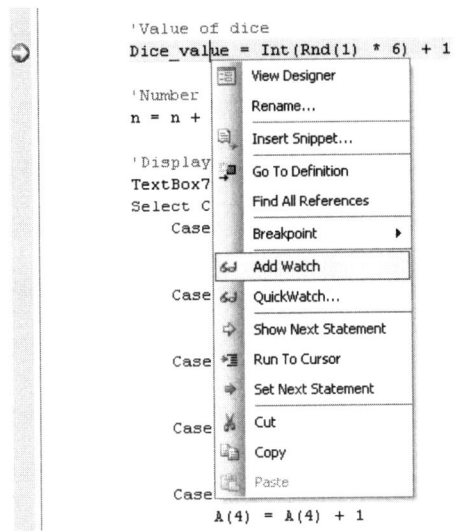

Figure 10.6 Adding a Watch window

Select *Add Watch* to obtain the selected variable placed in the Watch window (Figure 10.7).

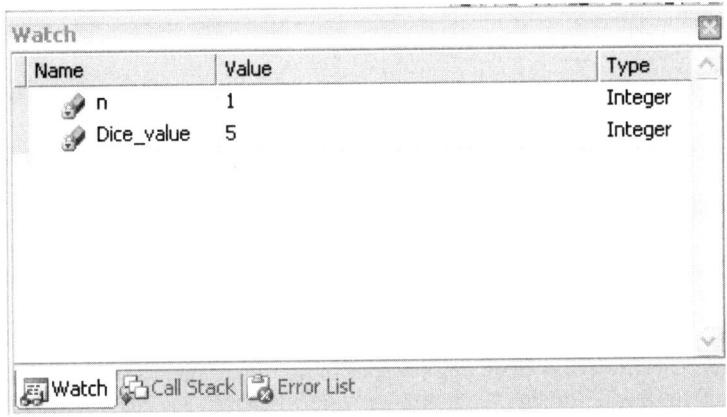

Figure 10.7 The Watch window

10 Debugging

Additional variables can be added by the drag-and-drop method. The variables can then be monitored as the program is run in the debugger mode using F5. Figure 10.8 shows how the variables can be monitored.

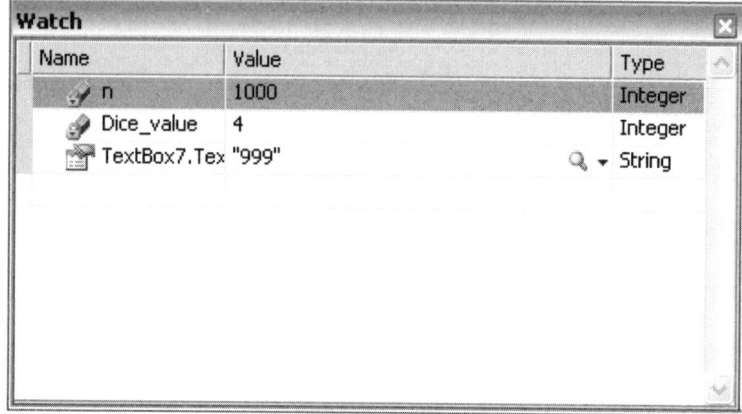

Figure 10.8 Monitoring the variables in the Watch window

Associated with the Watch Window is the Locals window. This window lists all the variables which are local to current procedure or functions. It can be displayed from **Debug>Windows** whilst in the paused Debugger mode and Figure 10.9 shows its contents.

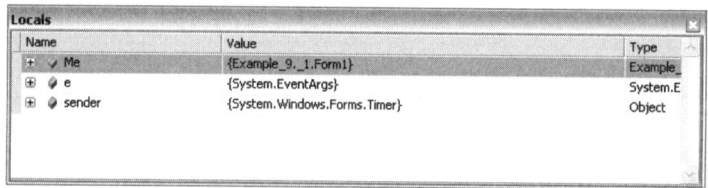

Figure 10.9 The Locals window

The Immediate Window

The Watch window does not always provide the full information that is required and there are times when you may feel that you wish to have a greater interaction with the program. You may feel that the program requires some more code or alternatively you are not getting a correct value for a variable. When the program is paused you can use the

Debugging 10

Immediate window. This is obtained from **Debug>Windows** and then select Immediate from the drop-down menu (Figure 10.10). Alternatively use **Ctrl+G**.

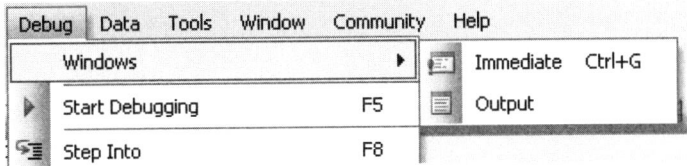

Figure 10.10 Obtaining the Immediate window

The Immediate window will then appear, either at the bottom of the IDE or floating (Figure 10.11).

Figure 10.11 The Immediate window

In this window you type in commands to obtain their immediate values. This is done when the program is in its paused state. The syntax used is *? Variable name.*

Figure 10.12 shows the results obtained when the program is paused and the values Dice_value and array A(4) are interrogated.

10 Debugging

Figure 10.12 The Immediate window in use

Summary

This chapter is important as it provides the transitional stage in the development of programming skills. The previous 9 chapters have laid the foundation of how to program Visual Basic 2005 Express and you have been led through programs that have systematically become more complex. This chapter has shown you some of the methods that are available within Visual Basic 2005 Express to debug programs. We have shown you the methods that involve adding textboxes and explained their advantages and disadvantages and we have also shown you how useful breakpoints in programs are. We have looked at *Watch* and *Immediate* windows and shown by example how they can be used.

The next stage is for you to start developing your own programs. Hopefully you will have acquired sufficient knowledge from this book to be able to write Visual Basic 2005 Express fluently but you can always return to these pages to remind you what to do prior to moving on to the more advanced books on the different editions of Visual Basic 2005 that are available.

Bibliography

This book has been designed to start you off in Visual Basic 2005 Express. To become more proficient in all versions of Visual Basic 2005 you must do real projects but you can learn so much more from other programmers. Here are a selection of other books which will help you. The list will start off with the ones that you should find easier to use, moving up to the ones which you need to be fairly expert to understand.

Michael Halverson, *Microsoft Visual Basic 2005 Step by Step*, 2005, Microsoft Press, ISBN 0-7536-2131-4

Evangelos Petroutsos, *Mastering Visual Basic 2005 Express Edition,* 2006, Sybex Inc, ISBN 0-7821-4398-9

Bill Sempf, *Visual Basic 2005 for Dummies*, 2006, Wiley Publishing Inc, ISBN 0-7645-7728-X

Thearon Willis & Bryan Newsome, *Beginning Visual Basic 2005,* 2005, Wrox, ISBN 0-7645-7401-9

James Foxall, *Sams Teach Yourself Visual Basic 2005 in 24 hours*, 2006, Sams, ISBN 0-6723-1836-9

Francesco Balena, *Programming Microsoft Visual Basic 2005*, 2006, Microsoft Press, ISBN 0-7356-2183-7

Bibliography

Appendix

What you learn from each Example

This Appendix is designed to give an overview of the different Examples that are introduced in each chapter. It shows the Form used for each Example, the Controls and Components, Variable types, Statements and Functions, and the Code which are used for the first time in that Example. Obviously each Example will build upon those features that you will have already encountered in previous ones.

The best way of learning how to program is to become familiar with reading the code and visualizing what happens as each line is processed. Here is your opportunity. Learn by reading code that is already written and know that it works.

Appendix

Example 2.1 My First Program

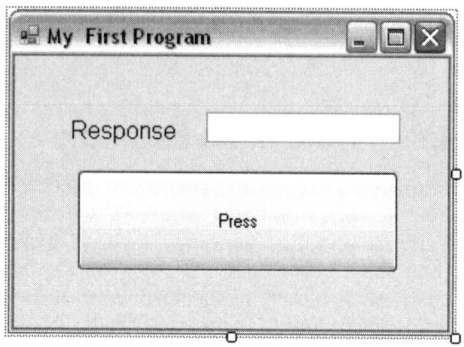

Controls/Components: Label1; TextBox1; Button1

Code

```
Public Class Form1

   Private Sub Button1_Click(ByVal sender As System.Object, ByVal e As System.EventArgs) Handles Button1.Click

      TextBox1.Text = "Hello World"
   End Sub
End Class
```

Example 3.1 Send & Receive

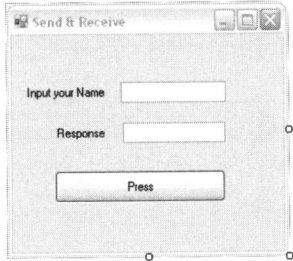

Controls/Components: Label1, 2; TextBox1, 2; Button1
Variables: Private, Public
Statements: Form_Load, Declarations

Code

```
Public Class Form1
  'Declare parameter
Private NA As String

   Private Sub Button1_Click(ByVal sender As Object, ByVal e As
System.EventArgs) Handles Button1.Click

     NA = TextBox1.Text
     TextBox2.Text = "Hello " + NA

   End Sub

   Private Sub Form1_Load(ByVal sender As Object, ByVal e As
System.EventArgs) Handles Me.Load

     TextBox1.Text = ""
     TextBox2.Text = ""

   End Sub
End Class
```

Appendix

Example 4.1 Scrollbar multiplier

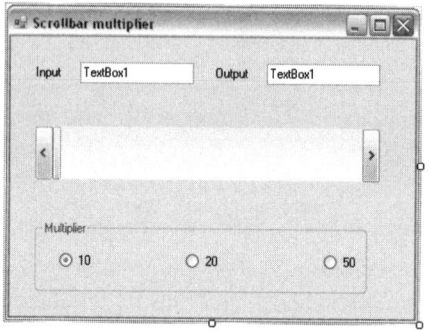

Controls/Components: Label1, 2; TextBox1, 2; HScrollbar1; GroupBox1; RadioButtons1, 2, 3

Code

```
Public Class Form1
  'Declare mult as integer variable
  Private mult As Integer

  Private Sub Form1_Load(ByVal sender As System.Object, ByVal e As System.EventArgs) Handles MyBase.Load

    'Initialise Multiplier to 10
    mult = 10

  End Sub

  Private Sub RadioButton1_CheckedChanged(ByVal sender As System.Object, ByVal e As System.EventArgs) Handles RadioButton1.CheckedChanged

    'Multiply by 10
    mult = 10

  End Sub

  Private Sub RadioButton2_CheckedChanged(ByVal sender As
```

Appendix

```
System.Object, ByVal e As System.EventArgs) Handles
RadioButton2.CheckedChanged

    'Multiply by 20
    mult = 20

End Sub

  Private Sub RadioButton3_CheckedChanged(ByVal sender As
System.Object, ByVal e As System.EventArgs) Handles
RadioButton3.CheckedChanged

    'Multiply by 50
    mult = 50

End Sub

  Private Sub HScrollBar1_Scroll(ByVal sender As System.Object,
ByVal e As System.Windows.Forms.ScrollEventArgs) Handles
HScrollBar1.Scroll

    'Place scrollbar value into Textbox
    TextBox1.Text = HScrollBar1.Value
    'Performmultiplier action
    TextBox2.Text = HScrollBar1.Value * mult

  End Sub
End Class
```

Appendix

Example 5.1 Random Numbers

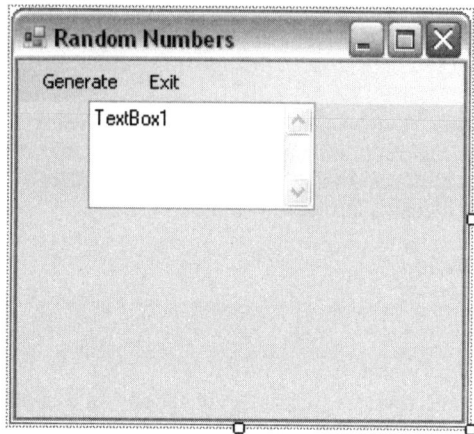

Controls/Components: MenuStrip1 (GenerateToolStripMenuItem, ExitToolStripMenu Item); Textbox1 (multiline)
Functions: Rnd(), Randomize(), Int()
Statements: For… Next, Catenization

Code

```
Public Class Form1

   Private Sub GenerateToolStripMenuItem_Click(ByVal sender As
System.Object, ByVal e As System.EventArgs) Handles
GenerateToolStripMenuItem.Click

     'Declare the variables
     Dim n As Integer
     Dim A As String
     Dim B$ = ""

     'Reseed random number generator
     Randomize()

     'For...Next loop
     For n = 1 To 100
        'store random number
```

Appendix

```
        A = Int(Rnd(1) * 100)
        'Add random number to character string
        B$ = B$ + A + ","
        'Display character string
        TextBox1.Text = B$
    Next

  End Sub

  Private Sub ExitToolStripMenuItem_Click(ByVal sender As
System.Object, ByVal e As System.EventArgs) Handles
ExitToolStripMenuItem.Click

      'End Project
      End

  End Sub
End Class
```

Appendix

Example 5.2 Random Numbers – timed

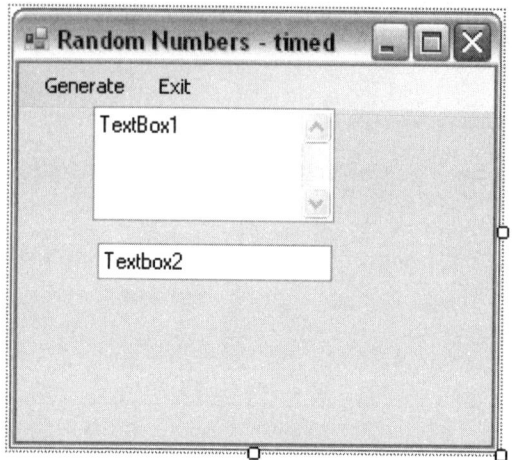

Controls/Components: MenuStrip1 (GenerateToolStripMenuItem, ExitToolStripMenu Item); Textbox1 (scrollbars); Timer1

Code

```
Public Class Form1

  'Declare variables
  Dim n As Integer
  Dim A As String
  Dim B$ = ""

  Private Sub GenerateToolStripMenuItem_Click(ByVal sender As
System.Object, ByVal e As System.EventArgs) Handles
GeneToolStripMenuItem.Click

    'Reseed random number generator
    Randomize()
    'Clear textbox
    TextBox1.Text = ""
    'Clear character string
    B$ = ""
    'Enable Timer
```

Appendix

```
    Timer1.Enabled = True
  End Sub

  Private Sub ExitToolStripMenuItem_Click(ByVal sender As
System.Object, ByVal e As System.EventArgs) Handles
ExitToolStripMenuItem.Click

    'End Project
    End

  End Sub

  Private Sub Timer1_Tick(ByVal sender As Object, ByVal e As
System.EventArgs) Handles Timer1.Tick

    'Increment counter
    n = n + 1
    'Display counter
    TextBox2.Text = n
    'store random number
      A = Int(Rnd(1) * 100)
      'Add random number to character string
      B$ = B$ + A + ","
      'Display character string
    TextBox1.Text = B$
    'Check counter
    If n > 9 Then
      'Disable counter
      Timer1.Enabled = False
      n = 0
    End If

  End Sub
End Class
```

Appendix

Example 6.1 Bitmap images

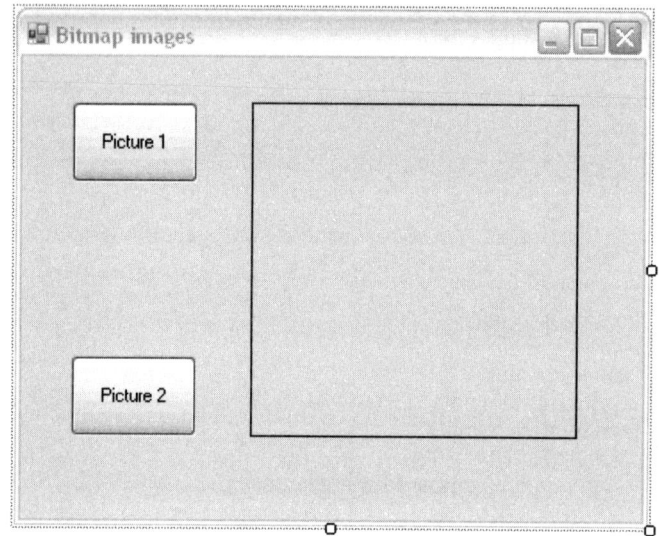

Controls/Components: PictureBox1; Button1, 2
Statements: PictureBox1.Image

Code

```
Public Class Form1

  Private Sub Button1_Click(ByVal sender As System.Object, ByVal e
As System.EventArgs) Handles Button1.Click

    'Load 501 x 427 bitmap image
    PictureBox1.Image = Image.FromFile("E:\VBProjects\logo.bmp")

  End Sub

  Private Sub Button2_Click(ByVal sender As System.Object, ByVal e
As System.EventArgs) Handles Button2.Click

    'Load 110 x 60 bitmap image
    PictureBox1.Image = Image.FromFile("E:\VBProjects\msdn.bmp")
```

Appendix

```
    End Sub
End Class
```

Appendix

Example 6.2 Icons

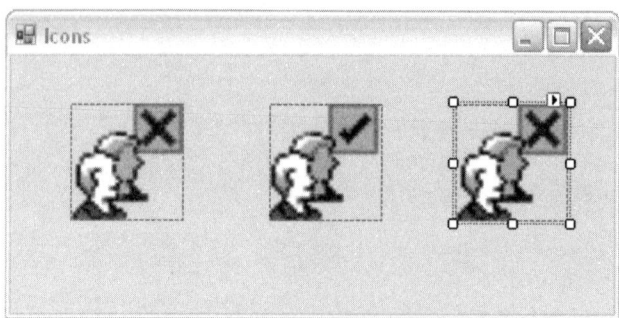

Controls/Components: PictureBox1, 2, 3 (Autosize)
Statements: PictureBox_Click

Code

```
Public Class Form1

  Private Sub PictureBox1_Click(ByVal sender As System.Object,
ByVal e As System.EventArgs) Handles PictureBox1.Click

    If PictureBox1.Image Is PictureBox2.Image Then
       PictureBox1.Image = PictureBox3.Image
    Else
       PictureBox1.Image = PictureBox2.Image
    End If

  End Sub
End Class
```

Example 6.3 Traffic lights

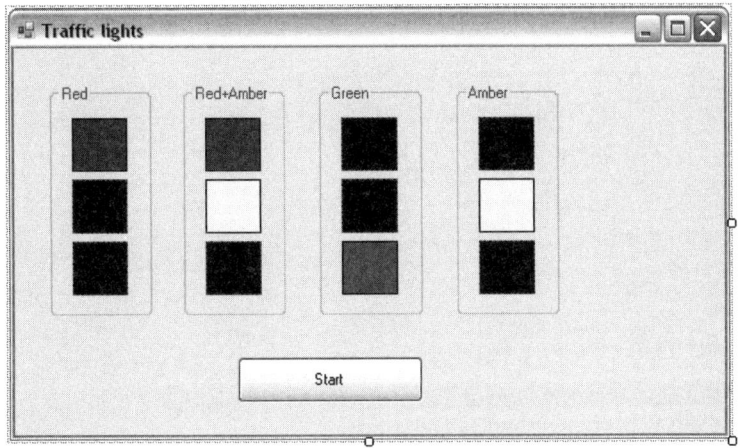

Controls/Components: GroupBox1, 2, 3, 4; PictureBox1 – 12; Button1
Statements: If..Else.. EndIf, Select Case

Code

```
Public Class Form1

  Dim n As Integer


  Private Sub Timer1_Tick(ByVal sender As System.Object, ByVal e As System.EventArgs) Handles Timer1.Tick

    'Increment counter
    n = n + 1
    'Change traffic light setting
    Select Case n

      Case 1
        'Red on, Amber on
        GroupBox1.Visible = False
        GroupBox2.Visible = True
      Case 2
        'Red off,Amber off, Green on
```

Appendix

```
            GroupBox2.Visible = False
            GroupBox3.Visible = True
        Case 3
            'Green off, Amber on
            GroupBox3.Visible = False
            GroupBox4.Visible = True
        Case 4
            'Amber off, Red on
            GroupBox4.Visible = False
            GroupBox1.Visible = True
            'Zero counter
            n = 0

    End Select

End Sub

Private Sub Form1_Load(ByVal sender As Object, ByVal e As System.EventArgs) Handles Me.Load

    'Initialise counter
    n = 0
    'Switch off clock
    Timer1.Enabled = False
End Sub

Private Sub Button1_Click(ByVal sender As System.Object, ByVal e As System.EventArgs) Handles Button1.Click

    'Check button status
    If Button1.Text = "Start" Then
        'Change button text
        Button1.Text = "Stop"
        'Switch on clock
        Timer1.Enabled = True
    Else
        'Change button text
        Button1.Text = "Start"
        'Switch clock off
        Timer1.Enabled = False
    End If

End Sub
End Class
```

Example 7.1 Graph axes

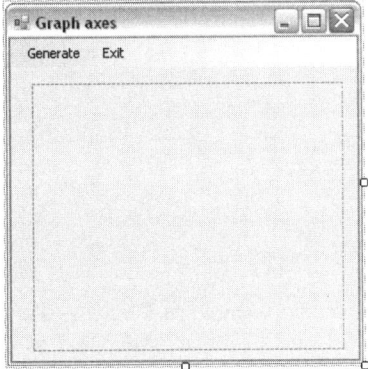

Controls/Components: MenuStrip1 (GenerateToolStripMenuItem, ExitToolStripMenu Item); PictureBox1
Statements: NewPen(), Drawline()

Code

```
Public Class Form1

  Private Sub GenerateToolStripMenuItem_Click(ByVal sender As
System.Object, ByVal e As System.EventArgs) Handles
GenerateToolStripMenuItem.Click

    'Declare graph variables
    Dim g As Graphics = PictureBox1.CreateGraphics
    Dim pen1 As New Pen(Color.Black)
    Dim n As Integer
    Dim j As Integer

    'Draw graph frame
    g.DrawLine(pen1, 0, 0, 250, 0)
    g.DrawLine(pen1, 250, 0, 250, 200)
    g.DrawLine(pen1, 250, 200, 0, 200)
    g.DrawLine(pen1, 0, 200, 0, 0)

    'Horizontal tick markers
    For n = 1 To 9
```

Appendix

```
      j = n * 25
      ' g.DrawLine(pen1, j, 200, j, 0)
      g.DrawLine(pen1, j, 200, j, 190)
    Next

    'Vertical tick markers
    For n = 1 To 9
      j = n * 20
      'g.DrawLine(pen1, 0, j, 250, j)
      g.DrawLine(pen1, 0, j, 10, j)
    Next

  End Sub

  Private Sub ExitToolStripMenuItem_Click(ByVal sender As
System.Object, ByVal e As System.EventArgs) Handles
ExitToolStripMenuItem.Click

    'End Program
    End

  End Sub
End Class
```

Appendix

Example 7.2 Sine wave graph

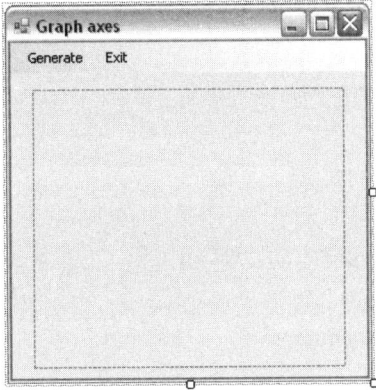

Controls/Components: MenuStrip1 (GenerateToolStripMenuItem, ExitToolStripMenu Item); PictureBox1
Function: Math.Sin()

Code

```
Public Class Form1

  Private Sub GenerateToolStripMenuItem_Click(ByVal sender As
System.Object, ByVal e As System.EventArgs) Handles
GenerateToolStripMenuItem.Click

    'Declare graph variables
    Dim g As Graphics = PictureBox1.CreateGraphics
    Dim pen1 As New Pen(Color.Black)
    Dim pen2 As New Pen(Color.Green)
    Dim n As Integer
    Dim j As Integer
    Dim y1 As Integer
    Dim y As Integer

    'Clear graph
    PictureBox1.Refresh()
    'Draw graph frame
    g.DrawLine(pen1, 0, 0, 250, 0)
    g.DrawLine(pen1, 250, 0, 250, 200)
```

Appendix

```vb
        g.DrawLine(pen1, 250, 200, 0, 200)
        g.DrawLine(pen1, 0, 200, 0, 0)

        'Horizontal tick markers
        For n = 1 To 9
           j = n * 25
           g.DrawLine(pen1, j, 200, j, 0)
        Next

        'Vertical tick markers
        For n = 1 To 9
           j = n * 20
           g.DrawLine(pen1, 0, j, 250, j)
        Next

        'Load first point data
        y1 = 100

        'Plot sine wave data
        For n = 0 To 250
           'Load sine wave data
           y = 100 - 100 * Math.Sin(2 * 3.142 * n / 250)
           'Plot points
           g.DrawLine(pen2, (n - 1), y1, n, y)
           'Store current data value
           y1 = y
        Next

    End Sub

    Private Sub ExitToolStripMenuItem_Click(ByVal sender As
System.Object, ByVal e As System.EventArgs) Handles
ExitToolStripMenuItem.Click

        'End Program
        End

    End Sub

End Class
```

Appendix

Example 7.3 Sine wave graph (Variable A & f)

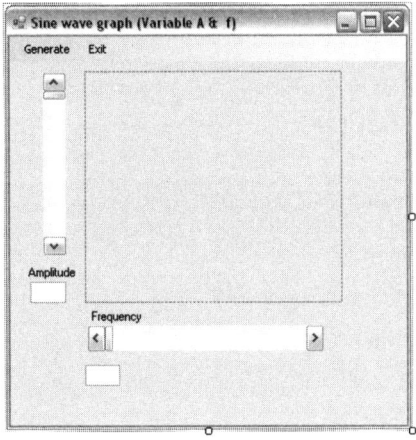

Controls/Components: Label1, 2; TextBox1, 2; MenuStrip1 (GenerateToolStripMenuItem, ExitToolStripMenu Item); PictureBox1; VScrollbar1, 2

Code

```
Public Class Form1

  Private Sub GenerateToolStripMenuItem_Click(ByVal sender As
System.Object, ByVal e As System.EventArgs) Handles
GenerateToolStripMenuItem.Click

    'Declare graph variables
    Dim g As Graphics = PictureBox1.CreateGraphics
    Dim pen1 As New Pen(Color.Black)
    Dim pen2 As New Pen(Color.Green)
    Dim n As Integer
    Dim j As Integer
    Dim y1 As Integer
    Dim y As Integer
    Dim Amp As Integer
    Dim Freq As Integer

    'Clear graph
```

Appendix

```vb
        PictureBox1.Refresh()
        'Draw graph frame
        g.DrawLine(pen1, 0, 0, 250, 0)
        g.DrawLine(pen1, 250, 0, 250, 200)
        g.DrawLine(pen1, 250, 200, 0, 200)
        g.DrawLine(pen1, 0, 200, 0, 0)

        'Horizontal tick markers
        For n = 1 To 9
           j = n * 25
           g.DrawLine(pen1, j, 200, j, 0)
        Next
        'Vertical tick markers
        For n = 1 To 9
           j = n * 20
           g.DrawLine(pen1, 0, j, 250, j)
        Next

        'Load first point data
        y1 = 100
        'Load amplitude
        Amp = VScrollBar1.Value
        'Load frequency
        Freq = HScrollBar1.Value

        'Plot sine wave data
        For n = 1 To 250
           'Load sine wave data
           y = 100 - Amp * Math.Sin(2 * 3.142 * n / Freq)
           'Plot points
           g.DrawLine(pen2, (n - 1), y1, n, y)
           'Store current data value
           y1 = y
        Next

    End Sub

    Private Sub ExitToolStripMenuItem_Click(ByVal sender As
System.Object, ByVal e As System.EventArgs) Handles
ExitToolStripMenuItem.Click

        'End Program
        End
```

Appendix

```vb
    End Sub

    Private Sub Form1_Load(ByVal sender As System.Object, ByVal e
As System.EventArgs) Handles MyBase.Load

        ' Display amplitude
        TextBox1.Text = VScrollBar1.Value
        'Display frequency
        TextBox2.Text = 1 / (HScrollBar1.Value / 250)

    End Sub

    Private Sub VScrollBar1_Scroll(ByVal sender As System.Object,
ByVal e As System.Windows.Forms.ScrollEventArgs) Handles
VScrollBar1.Scroll
        ' Display amplitude
        TextBox1.Text = VScrollBar1.Value

    End Sub

    Private Sub HScrollBar1_Scroll(ByVal sender As System.Object,
ByVal e As System.Windows.Forms.ScrollEventArgs) Handles
HScrollBar1.Scroll
        'Display frequency
        TextBox2.Text = 1 / (HScrollBar1.Value / 250)

    End Sub
End Class
```

Appendix

Example 7.4 Random number graph

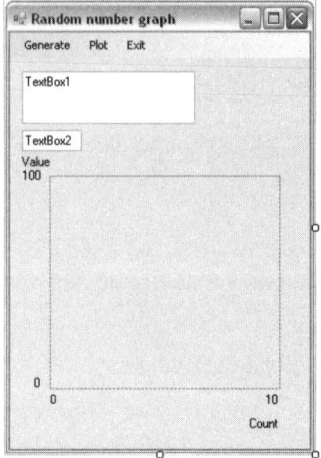

Controls/Components: Label1 – 17; TextBox1, 2; MenuStrip1 (GenerateToolStripMenuItem, PlotToolStripMenuItem, ExitToolStripMenu Item); PictureBox1
Statement: Array (Dim A())

Code

```
Public Class Form1
  'Declare the variables
  Dim n As Integer
  Dim A(11) As Integer
  Dim B$ = ""

  Private Sub GenerateToolStripMenuItem_Click(ByVal sender As
System.Object, ByVal e As System.EventArgs) Handles
GenerateToolStripMenuItem.Click

    'Reseed random number generator
    Randomize()
    'Enable timer
    Timer1.Enabled = True
    'Clear textbox
    TextBox1.Text = ""
```

Appendix

```vb
    'Clear character string
    B$ = ""
    n = 0

End Sub

Private Sub PlotToolStripMenuItem_Click(ByVal sender As
System.Object, ByVal e As System.EventArgs) Handles
PlotToolStripMenuItem.Click

    'Declare graph variables
    Dim g As Graphics = PictureBox1.CreateGraphics
    Dim pen1 As New Pen(Color.Black)
    Dim pen2 As New Pen(Color.Green)
    Dim j As Integer
    Dim y1 As Integer
    Dim y As Integer

    'Clear graph
    PictureBox1.Refresh()
    'Draw graph frame
    g.DrawLine(pen1, 0, 0, 250, 0)
    g.DrawLine(pen1, 250, 0, 250, 200)
    g.DrawLine(pen1, 250, 200, 0, 200)
    g.DrawLine(pen1, 0, 200, 0, 0)

    'Horizontal tick markers
    For n = 1 To 9
       j = n * 25
       g.DrawLine(pen1, j, 200, j, 0)
    Next

    'Vertical tick markers
    For n = 1 To 9
       j = n * 20
       g.DrawLine(pen1, 0, j, 250, j)
    Next

    'Make scales visible
    Label1.Visible = True
    Label2.Visible = True
    Label3.Visible = True
    Label4.Visible = True
```

Appendix

```
    'Load first point data
    y1 = 200 - 2 * A(0)

    'Plot random number data
    For n = 1 To 10
       'Load random number data
       y = 200 - 2 * A(n)
       'Plot points
       g.DrawLine(pen2, (n - 1) * 25, y1, n * 25, y)
       'Store current data value
       y1 = y
    Next

  End Sub

  Private Sub ExitToolStripMenuItem_Click(ByVal sender As
System.Object, ByVal e As System.EventArgs) Handles
ExitToolStripMenuItem.Click

    'End project
    End

  End Sub

  Private Sub Timer1_Tick(ByVal sender As System.Object, ByVal e
As System.EventArgs) Handles Timer1.Tick

    'Display counter
    TextBox2.Text = n
    'Store random number
    A(n) = Int(Rnd(1) * 100)
    'Add random number to character string
    B$ = B$ + Str$(A(n)) + ","
    'Display character string
    TextBox1.Text = B$
    'Increment counter
    n = n + 1
    'Check counter
    If n > 10 Then
       'Disable counter
       Timer1.Enabled = False
       n = 0
    End If
```

Appendix

```
    End Sub

    Private Sub Form1_Load(ByVal sender As System.Object, ByVal e
As System.EventArgs) Handles MyBase.Load
        'Clear textboxes
        TextBox1.Text = ""
        TextBox2.Text = ""

    End Sub
End Class
```

Appendix

Example 8.1 File writer

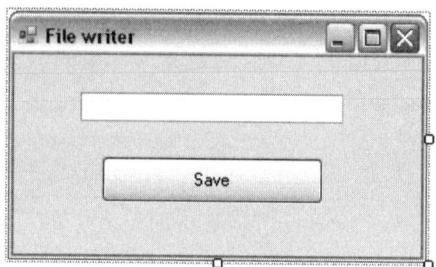

Controls/Components: TextBox1; Button1

Statements: SaveFile Dialog, dlgSave.Filter, dlgSave.ShowDialog

Code

```
Imports System.IO

Public Class Form1

  Private Sub Button1_Click(ByVal sender As System.Object, ByVal e As System.EventArgs) Handles Button1.Click

    'Declare filename variable
    Dim fname As String

    'Declare save file dialog
    Dim dlgSave As SaveFileDialog = New SaveFileDialog

    'Select save file dialog filter
    dlgSave.Filter = "Text Files|*.txt|All Files|*.*"

    'Open dialog and check if successful
    If dlgSave.ShowDialog = Windows.Forms.DialogResult.OK Then

      'Allocate filename
      fname = dlgSave.FileName
      'Prepare to transmit data stream
      Dim outstream As StreamWriter = New StreamWriter(fname)
```

Appendix

```vb
        'Read text box and send data to file
        outstream.WriteLine(TextBox1.Text)

        'Close file
        outstream.Close()

    End If

  End Sub
End Class
```

Appendix

Example 8.2 File reader

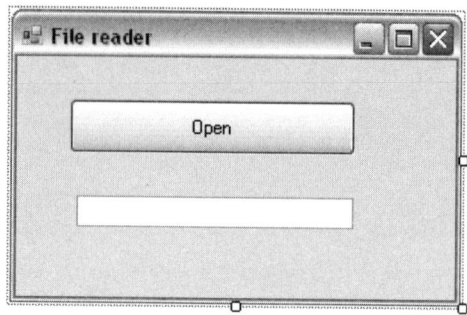

Controls/Components: TextBox1; Button1
Statements: OpenFile Dialog, dlgOpen.Filter, dlgOpen.ShowDialog

Code

```
Imports System.IO
Public Class Form1

  Private Sub Button1_Click(ByVal sender As System.Object, ByVal e As System.EventArgs) Handles Button1.Click

    'Declare filename variable
    Dim fname As String
    'Declare open file dialog
    Dim dlgOpen As OpenFileDialog = New OpenFileDialog

    'Select open file dialog filter
    dlgOpen.Filter = "Text Files|*.txt|All Files|*.*"

    'Open dialog and check if successful
    If dlgOpen.ShowDialog = Windows.Forms.DialogResult.OK Then

      'Allocate filename
      fname = dlgOpen.FileName

      'Prepare to receive data stream
      Dim instream As StreamReader = New StreamReader(fname)
```

Appendix

```
        'Data stream read from file and displayed
        TextBox1.Text = instream.ReadLine

        'Close file
        instream.Close()

    End If

  End Sub
End Class
```

Appendix

Example 8.3 Random number writer

Controls/Components: TextBox1; Button1, 2, 3

Statements: Chr(13) &Chr(10) (CR+LF), Header files
Functions: DateTime

Code

```
Imports system.io

Public Class Form1
   Dim j As Integer
   Dim num As Integer
   Dim A(10) As Integer
   Dim B As String


  Private Sub Button1_Click(ByVal sender As System.Object, ByVal e As System.EventArgs) Handles Button1.Click

     'Make B a null string
     B = ""

     'Loop
     For j = 0 To (num – 1)
        'Generate random number
        A(j) = Int(Rnd() * 100)
        'Add to string with CR & LF
```

Appendix

```vb
      B = B + Str(A(j)) & Chr(13) & Chr(10)
    Next

    'Display string
    TextBox1.Text() = B

  End Sub

  Private Sub Button2_Click(ByVal sender As System.Object, ByVal e
As System.EventArgs) Handles Button2.Click
    'Declare filename variable
    Dim fname As String

    'Declare save file dialog
    Dim dlgSave As SaveFileDialog = New SaveFileDialog

    'Select save file dialog filter
    dlgSave.Filter = "Text Files|*.txt|All Files|*.*"
    'Open dialog and check if successful
    If dlgSave.ShowDialog = Windows.Forms.DialogResult.OK Then

      'Allocate filename
      fname = dlgSave.FileName

      'Prepare to transmit data stream
      Dim outstream As StreamWriter = New StreamWriter(fname)

      'Transmit count number
      outstream.WriteLine(num)

      'Dimemension Date Time
      Dim myDate As DateTime = Now

      'Transmit Date & Time
      outstream.WriteLine(myDate)

      'Data loop
      For j = 0 To (num – 1)
        'Send data to file
        outstream.WriteLine(A(j))
      Next

      'Close file
      outstream.Close()
```

Appendix

```
    End If

End Sub

Private Sub Button3_Click(ByVal sender As System.Object, ByVal e As System.EventArgs) Handles Button3.Click

    'End program
    End

End Sub

Private Sub Form1_Load(ByVal sender As System.Object, ByVal e As System.EventArgs) Handles MyBase.Load

    'Number of random numbers to capture
    num = 10
    'Randomize the random number generator
    Randomize()

End Sub
End Class
```

Example 8.4 Random number reader

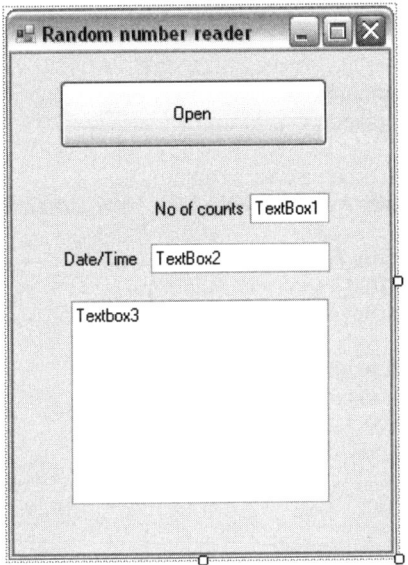

Controls/Components: Label1, 2, 3; TextBox1, 2, 3; Button1

Code

```
Imports System.io
Public Class Form1

   Private Sub Button1_Click(ByVal sender As System.Object, ByVal e As System.EventArgs) Handles Button1.Click

      'Declare variables
      Dim fname As String
      Dim j As Integer
      Dim B As String
      Dim num As Integer

      'Declare open file dialog
      Dim dlgOpen As OpenFileDialog = New OpenFileDialog
```

Appendix

```vb
        'Select open file dialog filter
        dlgOpen.Filter = "Text Files|*.txt|All Files|*.*"

        'Open dialog and check if successful
        If dlgOpen.ShowDialog = Windows.Forms.DialogResult.OK Then

            'Allocate filename
            fname = dlgOpen.FileName

            'Prepare to receive data stream
            Dim instream As StreamReader = New StreamReader(fname)

            'Read number count
            TextBox1.Text = instream.ReadLine
            num = TextBox1.Text

            'Read date and time
            TextBox2.Text = instream.ReadLine

            'Make B a null string
            B = ""

            'Loop
            For j = 0 To (num – 1)
                'Data stream read from file and displayed
                B = B + instream.ReadLine & Chr(13) & Chr(10)
            Next

            'Display data
            TextBox3.Text = B

            'Close file
            instream.Close()

        End If

    End Sub
End Class
```

Appendix

Example 8.5 Random number writer II

Controls/Components: Label1, 2, 3; TextBox1, 2, 3; Button1
Variables: Comma Separated Files (CSF)

Code

```
Imports system.io

Public Class Form1
    Dim j As Integer
    Dim A As Integer
    Dim B As String

    Private Sub Button1_Click(ByVal sender As System.Object, ByVal e As System.EventArgs) Handles Button1.Click

        'Make B a null string
        B = ""
        'Re-seed random number generator
        Randomize()

        'Loop
        Do Until A = 59
```

Appendix

```
        'Generate random number
        A = Int(Rnd() * 100)
        'Add to string with comma
        B = B + Str(A) + ","
    Loop

    'Display string
    TextBox1.Text() = B

End Sub

Private Sub Button2_Click(ByVal sender As System.Object, ByVal e As System.EventArgs) Handles Button2.Click

    'Declare filename variable
    Dim fname As String


    'Declare save file dialog
    Dim dlgSave As SaveFileDialog = New SaveFileDialog

    'Select save file dialog filter
    dlgSave.Filter = "Text Files|*.txt|All Files|*.*"

    'Open dialog and check if successful
    If dlgSave.ShowDialog = Windows.Forms.DialogResult.OK Then

        'Allocate filename
        fname = dlgSave.FileName

        'Prepare to transmit data stream
        Dim outstream As StreamWriter = New StreamWriter(fname)

        'Send data to file
        outstream.WriteLine(B)

        'Close file
        outstream.Close()

    End If

End Sub
```

Appendix

```
   Private Sub Button3_Click(ByVal sender As System.Object, ByVal e
As System.EventArgs) Handles Button3.Click
      'End program
      End

   End Sub

   Private Sub Form1_Load(ByVal sender As System.Object, ByVal e
As System.EventArgs) Handles MyBase.Load


   End Sub
End Class
```

Appendix

Example 8.6 Random number reader II

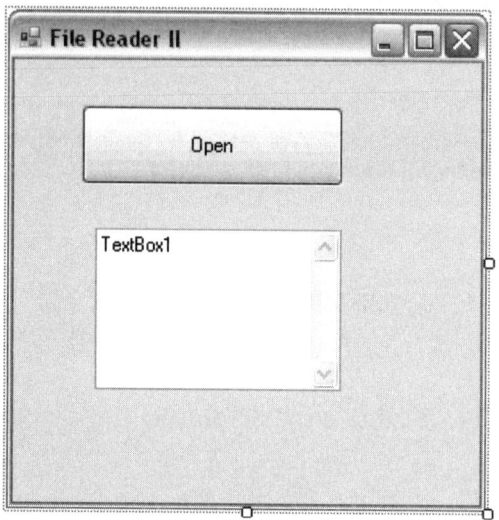

Controls/Components: TextBox1 (Scrollbar); Button1

Code

```
Imports System.IO

Public Class Form1

  Private Sub Button1_Click(ByVal sender As System.Object, ByVal e As System.EventArgs) Handles Button1.Click

    'Declare variables
    Dim fname As String
    Dim j As Integer
    Dim B As String

    'Declare open file dialog
    Dim dlgOpen As OpenFileDialog = New OpenFileDialog
```

Appendix

```vb
'Select open file dialog filter
dlgOpen.Filter = "Text Files|*.txt|All Files|*.*"

'Open dialog and check if successful
If dlgOpen.ShowDialog = Windows.Forms.DialogResult.OK Then

    'Allocate filename
    fname = dlgOpen.FileName

    'Prepare to receive data stream
    Dim instream As StreamReader = New StreamReader(fname)

    'Data stream read to end of file
    B = instream.ReadToEnd

    'Dimension variable as string and load data
    Dim Bstring As String = B

    'Display data after replacing commas with CR & LF
    TextBox1.Text = Bstring.Replace(",", Chr(13) & Chr(10))

    'Close file
    instream.Close()

  End If

 End Sub
End Class
```

Appendix

Example 9.1 Dice counter

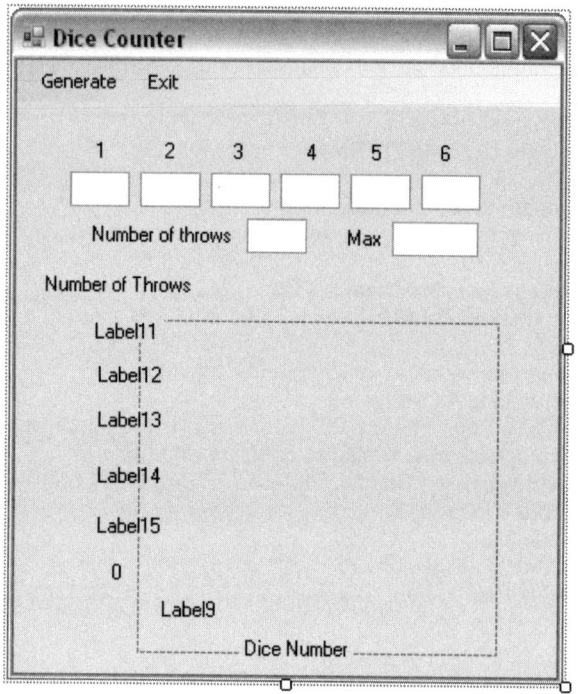

Controls/Components: Label1 – 17; TextBox1 – 8; MenuStrip1 (GenerateToolStripMenuItem, ExitToolStripMenu Item); PictureBox1

Code

```
Public Class Form1

    'Declare variables
    Dim A(5) As Integer
    Dim n As Integer
    Dim Dice_value As Integer
    Dim ymax As Integer
    Dim Amax As Integer
```

Appendix

```vb
Private Sub GenerateToolStripMenuItem_Click(ByVal sender As
System.Object, ByVal e As System.EventArgs) Handles
GenerateToolStripMenuItem.Click

    'Start timer
    Timer1.Enabled = True

End Sub

Private Sub Form1_Load(ByVal sender As Object, ByVal e As
System.EventArgs) Handles Me.Load

    'Zero counters
    A(0) = 0
    A(1) = 0
    A(2) = 0
    A(3) = 0
    A(4) = 0
    A(5) = 0

    'Display counters
    TextBox1.Text = A(0)
    TextBox2.Text = A(1)
    TextBox3.Text = A(2)
    TextBox4.Text = A(3)
    TextBox5.Text = A(4)
    TextBox6.Text = A(5)

    'Declare initialvalues
    ymax = 50
    Amax = 0

    'Hide chart labels
    Label9.Visible = False
    Label10.Visible = False
    Label11.Visible = False
    Label12.Visible = False
    Label13.Visible = False
    Label14.Visible = False
    Label15.Visible = False
    Label16.Visible = False
    Label17.Visible = False
    'Reseed random number generate
    Randomize()
```

Appendix

```
End Sub

Private Sub ExitToolStripMenuItem_Click(ByVal sender As Object,
ByVal e As System.EventArgs) Handles ExitToolStripMenuItem.Click

    'Switch off timer
    Timer1.Enabled = False

    'End program
    End

End Sub

Private Sub Timer1_Tick(ByVal sender As Object, ByVal e As
System.EventArgs) Handles Timer1.Tick

    'Value of dice
    Dice_value = Int(Rnd(1) * 6) + 1

    'Number of throws
    n = n + 1
    If n = 1000 Then
       n = 1001

    End If

    'Display number of throws
    TextBox7.Text = n
    Select Case Dice_value
       Case 1
          A(0) = A(0) + 1
          TextBox1.Text = A(0)
       Case 2
          A(1) = A(1) + 1
          TextBox2.Text = A(1)
       Case 3
          A(2) = A(2) + 1
          TextBox3.Text = A(2)
       Case 4
          A(3) = A(3) + 1
          TextBox4.Text = A(3)
       Case 5
          A(4) = A(4) + 1
```

Appendix

```vb
        TextBox5.Text = A(4)
     Case 6
        A(5) = A(5) + 1
        TextBox6.Text = A(5)
        'Plot graph
        Plotgraph()

  End Select

End Sub

Private Sub Plotgraph()

   'Declare graph variables
   Dim g As Graphics = PictureBox1.CreateGraphics
   Dim pen1 As New Pen(Color.Black)
   Dim n As Integer
   Dim j As Integer
   Dim x1 As Integer
   Dim y1 As Integer
   Dim xtemp As Integer
   Dim xxtemp As Integer
   Dim xlabel As String

   'Clear graphs
   PictureBox1.Refresh()

   'Initialise horizontal label
   xlabel = ""

   'Layout horizontal labels
   For j = 1 To 6
      xlabel = xlabel + Str(j) + Space(7)
   Next

   'Load horizontal labels
   Label9.Text = xlabel

   'Load vertical labels
   Label11.Text = ymax
   Label12.Text = Int(ymax * 4 / 5)
   Label13.Text = Int(ymax * 3 / 5)
   Label14.Text = Int(ymax * 2 / 5)
   Label15.Text = Int(ymax * 1 / 5)
```

Appendix

```
'Display labels
Label9.Visible = True
Label10.Visible = True
Label11.Visible = True
Label12.Visible = True
Label13.Visible = True
Label14.Visible = True
Label15.Visible = True
Label16.Visible = True
Label17.Visible = True

'Draw graph frame
g.DrawLine(pen1, 0, 0, 180, 0)
g.DrawLine(pen1, 180, 0, 180, 160)
g.DrawLine(pen1, 180, 150, 0, 150)
g.DrawLine(pen1, 0, 160, 0, 0)

'Horizontal tick markers
For n = 1 To 5
   j = n * 30
   g.DrawLine(pen1, j, 0, j, 160)
Next

'Vertical tick markers
For n = 1 To 4
   j = n * 30
   g.DrawLine(pen1, 0, j, 180, j)
Next

'Zero horizontal co-ordinate
x1 = 0

'Plot dice bar chart
For j = 0 To 5

   'Determine x-co-ordinate position
   xtemp = j * 10
   x1 = x1 + xtemp + 10

   'Determine y-height
   y1 = 150 - Int((A(j) / ymax) * 150)

   'Plot bar
```

Appendix

```
      For n = 0 To 10
         g.DrawLine(pen1, x1 + n, 150, x1 + n, y1)
      Next n

      'Determine next x co-ordinate
      xxtemp = j + 1
      x1 = 20 * xxtemp

      'Determine maximum values
      If A(j) > Amax Then
         Amax = A(j)

         'Display maximum values
         TextBox8.Text = Amax
      End If
    Next

    'Reset vertical axis maximum
    If Amax > ymax Then
       ymax = ymax + 50
    End If

  End Sub

  Private Sub Label13_Click(ByVal sender As System.Object, ByVal e As System.EventArgs) Handles Label13.Click

  End Sub
End Class
```

Appendix

Example 9.2 Colour mixing

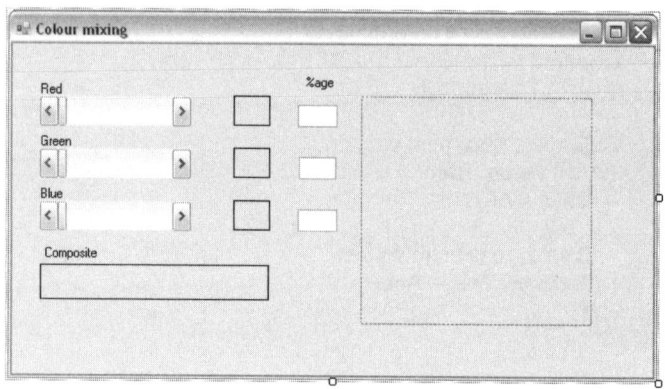

Controls/Components: Label1 – 5; TextBox1, 2, 3; PictureBox1 – 5; HScrollbar1, 2, 3

Code

```
Public Class Form1

  Private Sub HScrollBar1_Scroll(ByVal sender As System.Object,
ByVal e As System.Windows.Forms.ScrollEventArgs) Handles
HScrollBar1.Scroll

    'Red composition
    PictureBox1.BackColor = Color.FromArgb(255, HScrollBar1.Value,
    0, 0)

    'Red, Green, Blue mixture
    PictureBox4.BackColor = Color.FromArgb(255, HScrollBar1.Value,
    HScrollBar2.Value, HScrollBar3.Value)
    'Plot pie chart
    Pieplot()

  End Sub
```

Appendix

```vb
Private Sub HScrollBar2_Scroll(ByVal sender As System.Object, ByVal
e As System.Windows.Forms.ScrollEventArgs) Handles
HScrollBar2.Scroll

    'Green composition
    PictureBox2.BackColor = Color.FromArgb(255, 0,
    HScrollBar2.Value, 0)

    ' Red, Green, Blue mixture
    PictureBox4.BackColor = Color.FromArgb(255, HScrollBar1.Value,
    HScrollBar2.Value, HScrollBar3.Value)

    'Plot pie chart
    Pieplot()

End Sub

Private Sub HScrollBar3_Scroll(ByVal sender As System.Object,
ByVal e As System.Windows.Forms.ScrollEventArgs) Handles
HScrollBar3.Scroll

    'Blue composition
    PictureBox3.BackColor = Color.FromArgb(255, 0, 0,
    HScrollBar3.Value)
    'Red, Green, Blue mixture
    PictureBox4.BackColor = Color.FromArgb(255, HScrollBar1.Value,
    HScrollBar2.Value, HScrollBar3.Value)
    'Plot pie chart
    Pieplot()
End Sub

Private Sub Form1_Load(ByVal sender As System.Object, ByVal e
As System.EventArgs) Handles MyBase.Load

    'Set scroll bars to maximum
    HScrollBar1.Value = 255
    HScrollBar2.Value = 255
    HScrollBar3.Value = 255

    'Fill Picture boxes with colour
    PictureBox1.BackColor = Color.FromArgb(255, HScrollBar1.Value,
    0, 0)
    PictureBox2.BackColor = Color.FromArgb(255, 0,
    HScrollBar2.Value, 0)
```

Appendix

```
    PictureBox3.BackColor = Color.FromArgb(255, 0, 0,
    HScrollBar3.Value)
    PictureBox4.BackColor = Color.FromArgb(255, HScrollBar1.Value,
    HScrollBar2.Value, HScrollBar3.Value)

End Sub
Private Sub Pieplot()

    'Clear plotting area
    PictureBox5.Refresh()

    'Set up drawing parameters
    Dim g As Graphics = PictureBox5.CreateGraphics
    Dim pen1 As New Pen(Color.Red)
    Dim pen2 As New Pen(Color.Green)
    Dim pen3 As New Pen(Color.Blue)

    'Centre of pie chart co-ordinates
    Dim x1 = 100
    Dim y1 = 100

    'Declare variables
    Dim j As Integer
    Dim x2 As Integer
    Dim y2 As Integer

    Dim r0 As Integer
    Dim r1 As Integer
    Dim r2 As Integer

    Dim z As Integer

    Dim z0 As Integer
    Dim z1 As Integer
    Dim z2 As Integer

    Dim raverage As Integer

    'Obtain colour proportions
    r0 = HScrollBar1.Value
    r1 = HScrollBar2.Value
    r2 = HScrollBar3.Value
```

Appendix

```
'Average colour proportions
raverage = Int(((r0 + r1 + r2) / 3) * 100 / 255)

'Ensure radius average is non-zero
If raverage = 0 Then
   raverage = 1
End If

'Determine colour proportions
z0 = Int(r0 * 100 / raverage)
z1 = Int(r1 * 100 / raverage)
z2 = Int(r2 * 100 / raverage)

z = z0 + z1 + z2
If z = 0 Then
   z = 1
End If

'Convert colour proportions to degrees
r0 = Int(z0 * 360 / z)
r1 = Int(z1 * 360 / z)
r2 = Int(z2 * 360 / z)


'Plotting Red, Green, Blue pie chart

'Red proportion
For j = 0 To r0
   'x,y co-ordinates
   x2 = x1 + raverage * Math.Sin(2 * 3.142 * j / 360)
   y2 = y1 + raverage * Math.Cos(2 * 3.142 * j / 360)
   'Draw red line
   g.DrawLine(pen1, x1, y1, x2, y2)
Next

'Green proportion
For j = r0 To (r0 + r1)
   'x,y co-ordinates
   x2 = x1 + raverage * Math.Sin(2 * 3.142 * j / 360)
   y2 = y1 + raverage * Math.Cos(2 * 3.142 * j / 360)
   'Draw green line
   g.DrawLine(pen2, x1, y1, x2, y2)
Next
```

Appendix

```
    'Blue proportion
    For j = (r0 + r1) To (r0 + r1 + r2)
        'x,y co-ordinates
        x2 = x1 + raverage * Math.Sin(2 * 3.142 * j / 360)
        y2 = y1 + raverage * Math.Cos(2 * 3.142 * j / 360)
        'Draw blue line
        g.DrawLine(pen3, x1, y1, x2, y2)
    Next

    'Determine colour proportion percentages
    z0 = Int(z0 * 100 / z)
    z1 = Int(z1 * 100 / z)
    z2 = Int(z2 * 100 / z)

    'Display colour proportion percentages
    TextBox1.Text = z0
    TextBox2.Text = z1
    TextBox3.Text = z2

  End Sub

End Class
```

Index

A

All Files	119
Amplitude	102
Animation	78
Arrays	126
ASCII	118
AutoSize	76
Axes	96

B

Bitmap	71
BorderStyle	73, 163
Break All	175
Button	18

C

Cartesian graph	94
Case	51
Charts	145
Chr()	129
Chr(10)	128
Chr(13)	128
Classes	33
Close Project	25
Close()	120
Code window	33
Color	95, 151
Contents	126
Controls	32
Copy	78
CR	128
CreateGraphics	95, 151
CSF	117, 136
Currency	30

D

Date/Time	134
Debug Toolbar	174
Debugger	178
Debugging windows	178
Debugging	173
Declaration	37
Design time	43
DialogResult.OK	120
Dim	55
dlgOpen	124
dlgOpen.FileName	124
dlgOpen.Filter	124
dlgSave	119
dlgSave.Filter	119
Do Until…Loop	137
Double	30
DrawLine	96, 152
Dynamic Help	12

E

Error List	35, 142
Example 2.1	16, 186
Example 3.1	30, 187
Example 4.1	45, 188
Example 5.1	52, 190
Example 5.2	60, 110, 192
Example 6.1	72, 194
Example 6.2	78, 196
Example 6.3	84, 197
Example 7.1	96, 199
Example 7.2	103, 201
Example 7.3	105, 203
Example 7.4	111, 206
Example 8.1	119, 210
Example 8.2	123, 212
Example 8.3	127, 214
Example 8.4	132, 217
Example 8.5	136, 219
Example 8.6	140, 222
Example 9.1	145, 224
Example 9.2	162, 230
Excel	117, 145

Index

F

Files 71, 117
Font property 20
Font 20
For...Next 69
Form Load 47
Form 9
Form_Load 38
Frequency 102

G

Generate 53, 96, 127, 146
Graph 94
Graphics 73, 95, 151
Groupbox 45

H

Help 12, 74, 95, 173
High 102

I

Icon 71
IDE 4
Images 71
IMG 1
Immediate window 180
Installation 1
Instream 124
Integer 30
Integrated Development
  Environment 4
IO.StreamWriter 121
ISO 1

L

Label 18
Layout Toolbar 78
LF 128
Line drawing 95
Locals 180
Long 30
Loop 51
low 102

M

MainMenu 52
Math Class 103
Math.Sin 103, 168
MDI 6
Menu Bar 8
MenuItem 56
MenuStrip 52
Metafile 71
Method name box 38
Method Name 33
MSChart 93, 150
MSDN library 74, 173

N

New Pen 95, 151
New Project 3, 123
Notepad 123

O

Object 11
OpenFileDialog 124
Options 5
Outstream 120

P

Picture box 73, 93, 145
pieplot 166
Pixel 93
Private 24
Properties Window 7, 29
Public 37

R

Radio Buttons 44
Random numbers 131
Randomize 56
ReadToEnd 141
Replace 141
Rnd() 128
Run time 43
Run-time errors 173

236

Index

S

Save All	30
Save As	40
Save Project	31
Save	16
SaveFileDialog	119
Scale	94
SCDRESNL	80
SCDRESPL	82
Scrollbars	108
Select Case	87
Single	30
Size	78
Solution Explorer	7
Start Page	17
Start	2
Step Into	174
Step Out	177
Step Over	174
Stop Debugging	175
StreamWriter	119
String	30
String.Replace	141
Syntax errors	173
System.IO	118

T

Text Files	119
TextBox	57
Timer	51
Toolbar	6
Toolbox	7
Tool Windows	8
Tools	5
ToolStripMenuItem	55
Traffic lights	84

V

Variable parameter	29
View Class	33

W

Watch window	178
WriteLine	120